FOOD LOVERS' SERIES

Food Lovers' Guide to Houston

First Edition

The Best Restaurants, Markets &
Local Culinary Offerings

Kristin Finan

gpp

Guilford, Connecticut

Copyright © 2012 Morris Book Publishing, LLC

Editor: Kevin Sirois
Project Editor: Meredith Dias
Layout Artist: Mary Ballachino
Text Design: Sheryl Kober
Illustrations © Jill Butler with additional art by Carleen Moira Powell
Maps: Trailhead Graphics, Inc. © Morris Book Publishing, LLC

ISBN 978-0-7627-7313-8

Printed in the United States of America

10 9 8 7 6 5 4 3 2 1

All the information in this guidebook is subject to change. We recommend that you call ahead to obtain current information before traveling.

Contents

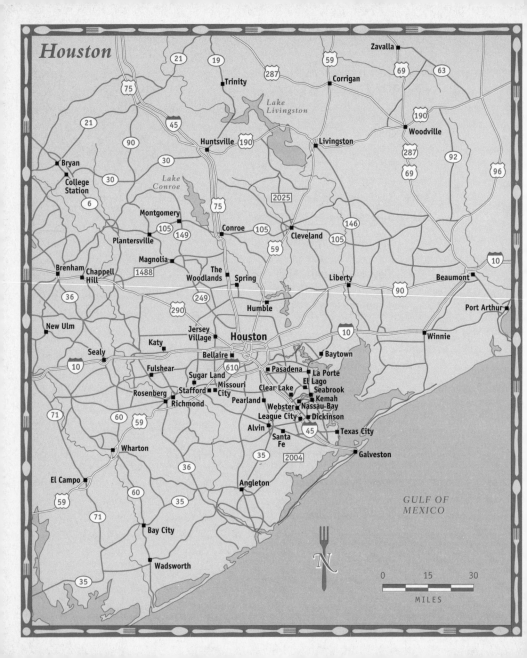

About the Author

Kristin Finan is an award-winning travel writer and author who particularly enjoys writing about her culinary adventures. This is her fourth book; her other books include *Quick Escapes from Houston* (Globe Pequot Press), *The Cheap Bastard's Guide to Houston* (Globe Pequot Press), and *The Cheap Bastard's Guide to Austin* (Globe Pequot Press). Her work regularly appears in the *Houston Chronicle,* one of the largest daily newspapers in the country, as well as in other national publications.

As a travel writer, Kristin has journeyed around the world, sampling dishes such as chile crab in Singapore, empanadas in Buenos Aires, and poutine in Montreal. She is happy to report that all three can be found in Houston.

When she's not traveling, you can find her continuing her search for the best crawfish in Texas with her husband, Patrick, and two daughters. She can be contacted at www.kristinfinan.com.

Acknowledgments

First, thanks to my husband, Patrick Badgley, and daughters Kona and Mirielle, who were by my side as we searched for the best *bahn mi*, burgers, and blueberry pie in the city. Your endless patience, boundless sense of adventure, and frank assessments of the places we visited made this a better book. I love you.

Thanks also to my parents, Jeanne and George, who suggested places I should try, babysat when I needed to go out late, and even convinced me to stay in for a few home-cooked meals when they sensed I could use a little downtime. All of your kind words and advice were more appreciated than you know.

Also, much appreciation to my friends and family who accompanied me to farmers' markets, barbecue shacks, and shaved-ice stands in the name of research, filled me in about their own personal dining disasters, or simply offered suggestions of places to go. Thanks in particular to Monica Haas, Rachel Gale, Brittney Mitchell, Keri Wiginton, Benjamin Finan, Cookie Roberts, Gina Finan, Shawn Badgley, Valerie Badgley, K. J. Joshi, Amora Rodrigues, Jen Samudio, and Tammy Portnoy. Thanks also to Lindsey Brown and the Greater Houston Convention and Visitors Bureau, which provided a wealth of ideas, and to Kevin Sirois, Amy Lyons, and the rest of the gang at Globe Pequot Press for the opportunity and support.

Finally, thanks to my stomach and my belt loops for their relentless can-do attitude.

Introduction

Full disclosure: I gained 30 pounds during the research of this book. Okay, I can't entirely blame the book—my research just happened to coincide with my second pregnancy. So you can believe me when I say that between the cravings and the incessant hunger, I took a major bite out of the Houston culinary scene.

I've always been a foodie in the making. Growing up, my day revolved around what my mom was cooking for dinner. From experimental dishes such as frittata and paella (typically requested by my brother, Benjamin, an even bigger foodie than I am) to favorites such as lasagna, enchiladas, and bouillabaisse, from night to night you never knew what was going to grace our kitchen table. My mom, a self-taught cook with a flair for the creative, can make anything—and I mean anything (expect maybe tripe—sorry, Mom)—taste incredible. Her motto: "You don't have to eat it all, but you at least have to try it."

Every holiday is a neighborhood affair at our house, as family and friends pour in to see what my mom will cook up next. Through her, I realized how good food can be and how to quickly spot when a dish is not living up to its potential.

So I was excited when I moved to Houston eight years ago and found that not only was it an international melting pot of cultures and people but that, as a result, it was also an international melting pot of cuisine. Of Houston's 2.3 million residents, 42 percent are white, 33 percent are Hispanic, 18 percent are African American, and 7 percent are Asian. Eighty-three languages are spoken in Houston, and international trade in some way supports more than one-third of the jobs in the area.

In recent years Houston has become an interesting, diverse, and high-profile mecca for foodies. Last year it was called "one of the most satisfying food scenes in the country" by the *New York Post* and a place "with a world-class food scene and a rising generation of culinary stars" by the *New York Times*.

Once you get to know a few of the key players—Bryan Caswell, Chris Shepherd, Monica Pope, Jonathan Jones—you start to get a feel for the special camaraderie you find here. On any given night you can find one high-profile chef at the bar of another high-profile chef's restaurant, swigging craft cocktails—another Houston specialty thanks to establishments such as Anvil Bar & Refuge—and swapping stories. On weekends those same chefs lead community members to their favorite hole-in-the-wall restaurants and dive bars as part of a highly popular "Where the Chefs Eat" program hosted by the Greater Houston Convention and Visitors Bureau.

Even more than individuals, though, it's the sense of community here that makes the culinary scene so special. When a very popular Vietnamese restaurant called Mai's burned down in an accidental fire in 2010, Houstonians stood outside the building and cried with the Nguyen family, who owned it. When the restaurant reopened in spring 2011, those same people poured in, eager to welcome back a Houston institution.

This is a community that cares about food and about the people who serve it up. I'm proud to live here. And more than happy to eat here.

How to Use This Book

This book has been organized into five chapters centered on geographical area. It starts in central Houston, which includes restaurants inside the I-610 Loop. Then we move on to north Houston, covering well-traveled areas such as The Woodlands, Spring, Tomball, and Humble. Those are followed by west Houston destinations, such as Sugar Land, Missouri City, Bellaire, and City Centre. Then we go to east Houston to check out areas such as Pearland, Pasadena, Clear Lake, and Seabrook. Finally we wrap up with the Houston outskirts: places such as Galveston, Bryan, and Brenham.

Price Code

Throughout the book you will see dollar signs to indicate how expensive a particular restaurant is. The restaurant price key applies to the price of an entree on the dinner menu; in many cases the price of lunch is significantly lower.

Here is the price code:

$	**Less than $10**
$$	**$10 to $20**
$$$	**$20 to $30**
$$$$	**More than $30**

Within each chapter you'll also find the following categories. Here's an explanation of each:

Foodie Faves

This category covers any restaurant, dive, shack, or food truck that is worth your time and money. It could be a diner that's been around forever or a brand-new bistro that's getting all the buzz. If it's in the area and you need to know about it, you'll find it here.

Landmarks

Landmarks are eateries that are well-known among Houstonians as must-try institutions. They are landmarks for different reasons—some have been part of the Houston restaurant scene for decades, while others are new but have quickly drawn widespread praise for their unique, innovative takes on food.

Specialty Stores, Markets & Producers

These sections may include anyone who makes something specific and makes it well. From specialty grocery stores to cake makers to sausage factories, if it's hard to find in Houston, you can probably find it in this category. Farmers' markets are included here.

Food Events

These events, most of which are annual, encompass the greatest food-related attractions around. Expect festivals, parades, fairs, workshops, and cooking classes, among others. You may want to sign up for some of these events in advance, however, as they can sell out.

Cocktail Culture

In addition to its food scene, Houston is also known for its incredible feats of alcohol, to the regular brews being turned out of the Saint Arnold Brewing Company to the ever-changing lists of craft cocktails at bars such as Anvil. If it comes in a keg, a bottle, or a 12-ounce can, you can probably find it listed here.

Getting Around

The city of Houston covers 634 square miles, which is large enough to contain the cities of New York, Washington, D.C., Boston, San

Francisco, Seattle, Minneapolis, and Miami. So it's only understandable that getting a feel for the lay of the land can take a while for visitors and residents alike.

The first thing you need to know is that you're going to need a car. The city spans so much space that it's nearly impossible to see everything without one. Sure, the MetroRail and bus system will do if they're your only option, but if you want to maximize your time, make sure you have a car at your disposal.

The city is divided by several major highways, including the I-610 Inner Loop (which includes downtown, the Museum District, and many of the major restaurants), the Beltway 8 Sam Houston Tollway (which circles the outer portion of the city), and I-45, I-10, and I-59. Knowing these five major thoroughfares will help a lot in terms of getting your bearings.

Keeping Up with Food News

Houston's food scene changes almost by the day. One minute a restaurant is so popular you have to wait weeks for a table; the next the attention has turned to the craft cocktail bar down the street. It's really hard to keep up, particularly with so many key players constantly making moves. If you want to try to keep up with the ever-changing flow, however, here are some websites you should bookmark.

Cleverley's Houston Restaurant News and Views, www
.cleverleysnewsletter.com. After the *Houston Post* newspaper closed
in 1995, Cleverley Stone found herself out of a job and ready to try
something new. So she began putting together a newsletter about
what was going on in Houston's restaurant, club, and hotel scenes
and sending it out to friends. Today she has turned into one of the
leading authorities on food in Houston.

CultureMap Houston, http://houston.culturemap.com. Calling
itself Houston's daily digital magazine, CultureMap Houston is dedicated to covering breaking news across all areas of Houston, from
fashion and music to politics and dining. And they do a darn good
job of it. The website's food and drink section regularly spotlights
changes in Houston's restaurant landscape, pop culture tidbits
about dining trends, and local favorites that are garnering national
attention.

Houston Chronicle, www.houstonchronicle.com. One of the
largest newspapers in the country, the *Houston Chronicle* covers the
Houston food scene from a variety of angles, from restaurant critic
Alison Cook's no-holds-barred reviews of the best and the worst
to fun foodie bites in entertainment magazine *29-95* (www.29-95
.com). Check the website often for news you need to know.

Houston Entree, www.houstonentree.com. Houston Entree con-
siders itself the "place where foodies connect," and with its wonderful deals, news, and awards, I'd say that holds pretty true. Check

this website to find the hottest deals and score an awesome price on your next designer dish.

Houston Press, www.houstonpress.com. Houston's alternative newsweekly is another authority on the Houston food scene, with regular articles about changes, openings, and scandals. Make sure to keep an eye on the online Eating Our Words blog, where the city's best and worst are written about every day.

Central Houston: Downtown and in the Loop

Geographically, Houston's Inner Loop—everything inside I-610, which circles the city—isn't that big of an area. But because it includes the downtown area as well as other popular districts such as Washington Avenue and Midtown, it is absolutely filled with wonderful restaurants. If you're going on a culinary adventure, this is where you will start. In fact, you could eat out here every day for a year and still not get a feel for everything that's available. There's just so much to see. Landmark restaurants such as Tony's and Niko Niko's can be found here, as well as new, cutting-edge restaurants that are making a splash in national newspapers and magazines. The variety here also spans the map, from mouthwatering Vietnamese cuisine to burgers that will change your life. Just be sure to check websites in advance for details on dress code, reservations, and

1

parking. Some of Houston's best-known places offer counter service, while others adhere to a strict jacket-and-tie policy.

In downtown, you're most likely to find upscale steak houses that offer great happy hour and lunch specials. Head to Washington Avenue and find a popular district for foodies absolutely brimming with new places to try. Some of them are incredible, others completely forgettable. From Rice Village, where trendy families enjoy bistro fare on sun-covered outside patios, to Midtown, where 20-somethings enjoy liquid meals and munch on fresh-baked tortilla chips and fresh-made salsa, there truly is something for everyone in the downtown and Inner Loop corridor.

Foodie Faves

Americas, 2040 W. Gray, Houston, TX 77056; (832) 200-1492; www.cordua.com; Latin American; $$$. Since the 1980s Michael Cordua has been a fixture in the Texas restaurant scene with restaurants such as **Churrascos, Artista,** and **Cordua.** Among my favorites of his brands is Americas, which offers fantastic food-forward Latin cuisine in a beautiful atmosphere. Don't miss the incredible ceviches, which range in type from ahi tuna to crab and shrimp to salmon, hand-crafted taquitos (plantain crusted shrimp is my favorite), and small plates that include empanadas, lobster corndogs, smoked lamb lollichops and corn-smoked crab fingers. In terms of entrees, choose from the churrasco steak, crispy pork carnitas, or grilled chicken breast with organic quinoa grilled asparagus and avocado mousse, among others. An additional location is 21 Waterway Ave. in The Woodlands. For Chef David Cordua's recipe for **Crab and Shrimp Ceviche,** see p. 190.

Backstreet Cafe, 1103 S. Shepherd Dr., Houston, TX 77019; (713) 521-2239; www.backstreetcafe.net; American; $$. You can expect Backstreet Cafe, part of the legendary Hugo's chain, to be good. And it is. Serving "seasonal American cuisine," Backstreet Cafe is located in a beautiful, inviting space that makes you want to linger. And the menu here is worth lingering over. Start with the delightful asparagus and mushroom tart or some duck spring rolls paired with one of the many wines offered here. Follow that up with a cup of Gulf Coast filé gumbo or ratatouille salad. Then choose between diverse and decadent main entrees that include jalapeño fettuccine, coffee-crusted tenderloin, braised short ribs, hash of slow-roasted lamb shoulder, curried coconut seafood soup, and a vegetarian platter. Brunch, lunch, and a special vegetarian menu are also offered.

Barnaby's, 604 Fairview, Houston, TX 77006; (713) 522-0106; www.barnabyscafe.com; Breakfast; $$. This dog-themed cafe is among Houstonians' favorite places to grab lunch or dinner thanks to its reliable food and festive atmosphere. You may have to wait during busy times on the weekend, but it's always worth it for an order of perfectly cooked waffle fries with blue cheese fondue, a heaping turkey sandwich with cranberry mayo, or what I consider to be the best veggie burger in Houston. There's also a full breakfast menu that includes items such as a petite steak with eggs, grits or potatoes, and a biscuit and wheat toast; buttermilk pancakes; and a breakfast burrito with scrambled eggs, black beans, and Monterey Jack cheese with potatoes and salsa on the side. Additional locations are at 5750 Woodway Dr., 1701 S. Shepherd, and 414 W. Gray.

Beaver's, 2310 Decatur St., Houston, TX 77007; (713) 864-2328; www.beavershouston.com; Barbecue; $$. This is a good place to go for many reasons—the nice outside patio, the innovative cocktail selection—but the food here is the major draw. With well-known Executive Chef Jonathan Jones showcasing his "passion for all things rubbed, aged, smoked, and slow-cooked," you know the fare here is going to be worth writing home about. I've come to love the food here, which manages to be both completely satisfying and completely surprising every time I visit. The starters offer little bites of innovation, ranging from Big Fried Balls (house-made boudin balls with smokin' green remoulade) to Nacho Mama's Oysters (Texas cornmeal-crusted oysters with guacamole and smoky habañero salsa on locally made flour-tortilla crisps) to fried green tomatoes. For entrees, consider smoked pork ribs, Texas longhorn meat loaf, a Pit Boss Chickwich (sloppy shredded barbecue chicken with a fried egg, crispy cornmeal, onions, coleslaw, and a pickle), or the famous Beaver Burger (a patty of sirloin, brisket, and bacon served with chips, lettuce, onion, and tomato).

Benjy's, 5922 Washington Ave., Houston, TX 77007; (713) 868-1131; www.benjys.com; American; $$. Need a date night out with your sweetie? I highly recommend Benjy's, where the fruit-flavored martinis flow like water and the Asian-inspired American fare never fails to impress. Start with a drink at the glossy upstairs bar, then move downstairs to nosh on menu items that include bacon potato pizza, wood oven–roasted half chicken, seared scallops with forbidden black rice, Milton's warm 10-vegetable salad, and nearly half a dozen pizzas. In more of a snacking mood? Try the house-cured salmon sashimi, roasted portobello crepes, pork pot stickers, or fried brussels sprouts. Lunch, brunch, happy hour, and Sunday supper menus are also offered. A second location is at 2424 Dunstan in Rice Village.

Berryhill Baja Grill, 702 E. 11th St., Houston, TX 77008; (713) 225-2252; www.berryhillintheheights.com; Tex-Mex; $$. Let's start with one word: tamales. That's what this local chain of restaurants is known for, and no matter what kind you order—from the tender spinach and corn to the fall-apart chicken—you can't go wrong. They even serve up special-occasion tamales throughout the year, such as turkey tamales with a side of gravy around Thanksgiving. But more than that, this popular Heights restaurant offers combination platters, fabulous quesadillas, delicious guacamole, and perfectly crafted margaritas. You should be warned that if you go for an early dinner, particularly on a weekend, the place is absolutely swarming with kids, but if you go later you should find a more subdued crowd. Either way, you'll enjoy the laid-back counter service, the chips and salsa, the wide outside patio, and the menu. Other can't-miss menu items include the *queso* with shrimp, the award-winning fried fish tacos, a beef or chicken fajita platter, cheese enchiladas topped with red jalapeño sauce, and pico de gallo and mushroom poblano quesadillas. Breakfast is also served here: Options include breakfast tacos, *migas,* and *chilaquiles.*

Bistro Lancaster, 701 Texas St., Houston, TX 77002; (713) 228-9500; www.thelancaster.com; American; $$$. My nights at Bistro Lancaster always begin and end with Champagne. I'm not sure why that is, but I have a feeling it has to do with the festive atmosphere that radiates here, whether you go on a Monday or a Friday. Located inside the boutique Lancaster Hotel in the heart of downtown right next to the theater district, Bistro Lancaster serves up American classics that include baked oysters with Gorgonzola, parsley, and red pepper coulis; beef carpaccio with baby arugula, mushroom confit, balsamic vinegar, and olive oil; Tuscan scallops with gnocchi, crispy pancetta, sautéed arugula, mushrooms, tomatoes, and shallots with lobster emulsion; and a grilled pork chop with roasted fingerling potatoes, grilled asparagus, and serrano ham cream sauce. Breakfast, brunch, and lunch are also served. And don't miss the incredible dessert offerings, which include bread pudding with brandied dried cherries, fig confit, and caramel sauce; Rose's key lime torte with raspberry compote and whipped cream; and the out-of-this-world peach panna cotta with fresh peach puree and a mint reduction.

Bombay Brasserie, 2414 University Blvd., Ste. 210, Houston, TX 77005; (713) 355-2000; www.thebombaybrasserie.com; Indian; $$. Rice Village has long been one of my favorite areas in Houston for its bustling shops, restaurants, and walkable spaces. After a full day of shopping, you will have worked up a pretty good appetite—that's when you should stop into Bombay Brasserie. The selection of traditional Indian cuisine is stellar, and the staff is consistently warm and inviting. Not sure what you want? Drop by for the daily lunch buffet, which includes staples such as samosas, naan, *saag paneer,* chicken tikka masala, and more. Want more control over your meal? Go for dinner, when you can select from a menu brimming with options such as a Bombay vegetable platter (vegetable *pakoras,* samosas, *aloo tikki,* and cheese *pakoras*); lamb tenderloin with ginger, garlic, potatoes, and yogurt; mahimahi masala; and chicken vindaloo. With more than a dozen vegetarian options, non–meat eaters will also go home happy. Oh, and don't forget to try a scoop of mango or pistachio ice cream for dessert. A second location is at 3005 W. Loop South.

Bombay Pizza Co., 914 Main St., Ste. 105, Houston, TX 77002; (713) 654-4444; www.bombaypizzaco.com; Indian; $$. Here's what's cool about this place: They serve up top-notch pizza with toppings inspired by traditional Indian ingredients. Sounds strange? Trust me, it works. Options here include the Slumdog (pepperoni, Spanish chorizo, beef, Canadian bacon, mozzarella, garlic chicken, jalapeños, and red onion), Sonu's Rita (basil, tomato, mozzarella, *paneer,* and cilantro-mint chutney), Gateway of India (tandoori chicken, crabmeat, artichoke hearts, fresh cilantro, mozzarella, provolone, and cilantro-mint chutney), and *saag paneer* (collard greens and spinach, *paneer,* fontina, goat cheese, and mozzarella). You should be warned that the crust is prepared super thin (which I love); pizza by the slice is available during lunch. With its prime downtown location (and easy access from the MetroRail system), it's a must-try for anyone who likes pizza mixed with a little innovation.

Boom Boom Room, 2518 Yale St., Houston, TX 77008; (713) 868-3740; www.theboomboomroomhouston.com; Wine Bar; $$. Ever just feel like relaxing with a good bottle of wine, a delicious panini, and some fantastic jazz? Why stay in? Head to the Boom Boom Room, where an upbeat atmosphere meets truly delicious food at a place you'll want to visit over and over again. Want something a little more unique than wine? Check out the list of Champagne cocktails or order a glass of wonderful sangria. The restaurant is open Tues through Sat from 4 p.m. to 2 a.m. Closed Sun and Mon.

Boudreaux's Cajun Kitchen, 5475 W. Loop South, Houston, TX 77081; (713) 838-2200; www.boudreauxs.net; Cajun; $$. You can find tasty Cajun food throughout Houston, and if you're craving some good stuff, Boudreaux's Cajun Kitchen is always a safe bet. A local chain that originated in Houston, Boudreaux's features all the best dishes you've come to know and love. Expect boudin balls, fried pickles, seafood fondue, gumbo, jambalaya, red beans and rice, shrimp and crawfish étouffée, po'boys, and dirty rice, to name a few. Gluten-free menu options are also available. The pastas, too, are a standout: I like the pasta jambalaya with shrimp, chicken, sausage, onions, and bell peppers in spicy Cajun sauce. And since this one is located in the Galleria area, it's a good place to satisfy your hunger after an afternoon shopping excursion. Other Houston area locations are also available.

Branch Water Tavern, 510 Shepherd, Houston, TX 77007; (713) 863-7777; www.branchwatertavern.com; American; $$$. Branch Water Tavern calls itself a modern American tavern, and I'd say that's a pretty apt description of the top-notch food and innovative drinks this restaurant regularly serves up. Some of my favorite menu items here include pan-roasted Bryan Farms chicken with gnocchi, market vegetables, and thyme jus; Oregon Dover sole with artichokes, spring vegetable ragout, and *pistou* broth; Berkshire pork chop with succotash and bacon bouillon; and venison medallions with sweet potato and brussels sprouts hash, bacon confit, and pomegranate jus. Not that hungry? Try sharing a plate of

The Houston Food Truck Scene

The food truck scene has exploded around the country in recent years, and Houston is no exception. If you like to eat lunch served out the window of miniature Airstream trailer or the like, here are four places you can't miss. For a regularly updated report on the scene in Houston, check out **www.houstonfoodtrucks.com.**

Bernie's Burger Bus
Though this one may be known for its interesting exterior—it's housed inside a yellow school bus—Bernie's Burger Bus is even better known for the delectable burgers it serves up, made from black Angus beef, local cheddar cheese, and homemade condiments.
Menu offerings include The Bully (2 signature patties with cheddar, mayo, mustard, ketchup, pickle, thin sliced onions, shredded lettuce, and slow-roasted garlic tomatoes), Detention (2 applewood-smoked bacon grilled cheeses used as a bun with 2 signature beef patties topped with cheddar cheese, onions, and all the fixings), and Homeroom (a burger served with applewood-smoked bacon, cheddar, onions, and chipotle aioli, and topped with a fried egg). Location varies by day; check www.berniesburgerbus.com for details.

Good Dog Hot Dogs
Think local artisan buns, hand-crafted condiments, and Texas-made all-natural franks. Sounds pretty good, right? It is. Good Dog Hot Dogs serve up a variety of consistently good hot dogs—toppings may include bacon, cream cheese, jalapeño relish, and pickled onions—in perfectly toasted buns. Track down the truck's current location at www.gooddogfoodtruck.com.

Melange Creperie
Okay, this isn't a truck so much as a dude standing at a cart. Chances are good you'll flip anyway at this delicious crepe stand open Mon, Thurs, and Fri from 7 a.m. to 1 p.m. and weekends from 10 a.m. to 2 p.m. at Westheimer and Taft in the Montrose district. Crepe varieties include egg, ham, and cheese; strawberry with fresh-picked figs; and chicken with goat cheese. Find out more at http://twitter.com/MelangeCreperie.

Oh My Pocket Pies
Like empanadas? Then you'll love this place, which was one of the early arrivals to the Houston food truck scene. Expect golden pastry dough stuffed with anything from twice-baked potato to pulled pork to s'mores ingredients. Trust me—they're delicious. Find out more at www.ohmypocketpies.com.

perfectly crafted charcuterie or steamed mussels, or grab some duck-fat popcorn or pork *rillettes* biscuits. The bacon-wrapped Gulf shrimp appetizer with grits and a slow-poached egg is another favorite. Brunch, lunch, and happy hour menus are also offered. For Chef David Grossman's recipe for **Peach Tart Tatin,** see p. 204.

Brasil, 2604 Dunlavy St., Houston, TX 77098; (713) 528-1993; Breakfast; $$. Despite the many options, it took me awhile to find a place in Houston that I loved for a late breakfast. When I finally made my way to Brasil, I fell instantly in love. The sparse decor, wide coffee bar, and tantalizing menu made me feel like I was in the right place. My favorite order remains a slice of quiche with a side salad, but the fare is much more varied than that, with pizzas, sandwiches, soups, and salads that will make your mouth water. Don't miss the heart of palm sandwich here—it's a Houston treasure. There's also a great beer and wine selection, and frequent live music. If the weather's nice, be sure to grab a seat on one of the outside patios.

Brasserie Max and Julie, 4315 Montrose Blvd., Houston, TX 77006; (713) 524-0070; www.caferabelais.com/Brasserie/Home .html; French; $$$. From the outside this place looks like a charming bistro you'd see along the streets of Paris. Once you sit down, you learn that the food is like something out of Paris as well—smart, perfectly cooked dishes that will leave you craving more. It's casual, warm, and inviting, particularly for weekend brunch (held from 11 a.m. to 3 p.m.), when fare such as sweet and savory crepes, waffles, omelets, *croque-monsieur*, and *croque-madame* grace the menu. There's also a full wine list and a dinner menu with all your French favorites, such as house-made pâté, roasted bone marrow, bouillabaisse, and a variety of cheeses imported from France. Eat it with the bread that's served fresh to your table once you sit down—it's incredible. But if you go for only one thing, go for the crepes, which are wonderful.

Brasserie 19, 1962 W. Gray, Houston, TX 77019; (713) 524-1919; www.brasserie19.com; French; $$$. If you know the Houston food scene at all, you know what a prominent role **Ibiza** restaurant (see p. 33) plays in it. Now the owners of Ibiza have opened a new venture described as "French classicism meets modern luxury." Expect wonderful, hearty French country fare such as hand-cut steak tartare, roasted young hen, filet mignon, and Gulf Coast bouillabaisse, as well as Texas-inspired favorites such as Gulf red snapper, American osetra caviar, and Texas sweet onion soup. Daily specials such as sautéed true Dover sole (Wednesday) and cassoulet (Sunday) are also available. Open daily. Sunday brunch, which includes dishes such as watercress salad, house-made granola, and Burgundy escargot gratin, is also served.

BRC Gastropub, 519 Shepherd Dr., Houston, TX 77007; (713) 861-2233; www.brcgastropub.com; American; $$$. I have to admit that I was originally underwhelmed by this establishment, which when it first opened made a big splash thanks to its cheeky name. (BRC stands for Big Red Cock, a tribute to the giant statue of a red rooster that stands outside.) Over time, however, it has won me over with its inventive menu and extensive beer and wine lists. The cuisine here is considered creative, pub-inspired American fare that can range from whimsical to hard-to-find. Among my favorite menu items: fresh-baked bacon cheddar biscuits, steak-fried mushrooms with red pepper jam, barbecued salmon Cobb salad, the brisket supper open-face sandwich, State Fair Griddled Cheese, and the BRC pub burger. Sides include avocado blue cheese potato salad, sour cream mashed potatoes, asparagus with bacon jam and butter, and garlicky sautéed young spinach. Brunch is served starting at 10 a.m. on weekends; reservations are accepted.

Brenner's on the Bayou, 1 Birdsall St., Houston, TX 77007; (713) 868-4444; www.brennerssteakhouse.com; Steak House; $$$. The first thing that will strike you about this restaurant, located on Buffalo Bayou, is its incredible patio, where lush greenery and a cascading waterfall take you far away from Houston. The next thing you'll notice about this Landry's-owned restaurant is that the menu is top-notch, featuring delicious steaks ranging in size from 6 to 22 ounces. The menu also features other fantastic entrees, such as short-rib ravioli, porcini roasted chicken, and Chef's Land & Sea (Jack Daniel's–smoked Berkshire pork short rib paired with fresh Gulf snapper with jalapeño smoked cheddar mashed potatoes). The appetizers, too, are worth a good look. I'm particularly fond of the house-made pretzels, pan-roasted shrimp, and beef carpaccio served with wilted greens, Parmesan cheese, and sun-dried tomato vinaigrette. Dinner is served daily; a Sunday brunch is also available.

Buffalo Grille, 4080 Bissonnet St., Houston, TX 77005; (713) 661-3669; www.thebuffalogrille.com; Breakfast; $$. Breakfast is the name of the game at this well-known establishment, where must-try items include pancakes filled with your choice of items such as strawberries, blueberries, bananas, raspberries, apples, peaches, raisins, pecans, or (my favorite) chocolate chips; a huevos burrito with scrambled eggs, sausage, and beans topped with cheese and ranchero or green chile sauce; and build-your-own omelets featuring ingredients such as potatoes, black olives, jalapeños, bacon, guacamole, and cheese. Lunch and dinner are also served and include offerings such as chicken quesadillas, peppered pork chops, baked potatoes, grilled bacon and cheese, and, fittingly, a buffalo burger. Call ahead to find out the vegetable of the day. A second restaurant is located at 1301 S. Voss Rd.

Cafe Moustache, 507 Westheimer Rd., Houston, TX 77006; (713) 524-1000; www.cafemoustache.com; French; $$$. Let's cut right to the chase: This cozy neighborhood bistro is absolutely fantastic, serving up French country comfort food that rivals anything you'd find in France. The restaurant claims its food would have made "Julia Child weak in the knees," and, to be honest, I think they're right. Start with a perfectly prepared appetizer, such as truffle fries, smoked salmon profiteroles, or bacon-wrapped Texas quail, followed by a tuna niçoise salad, escargots de Bourgogne, or pâté de campagne. For a main course, consider *truite meunière* (rainbow trout fillet with butter, parsley, and lemon juice), shrimp *pernod* (fresh Gulf shrimp sautéed with garlic butter and herbs), or *medaillons de porc* (seared pork loin medallions with vegetables and lyonnaise potatoes). And that's just the dinner menu. Lunch fare is similar but includes items such as quiche lorraine and baguettes du jour. There's also a delectable Sunday brunch—including a $14.95 three-course prix-fixe option—and special events such as happy hour, with $4 hors d'oeuvres and $5 wine, and occasional wine dinners.

Cedar Creek Cafe Bar & Grill, 1034 W. 20th St., Houston, TX 77008; (713) 808-9623; www.cedarcreek.squarespace.com; American; $$. Whenever we can't figure out where to go for lunch, we always end up here because of the varied, scrumptious fare and impressive cocktail and beer selection. Part of a chain of 4 local restaurants, Cedar Creek has a laid-back vibe with counter service and a huge outside patio space, allowing it to be both kid-friendly and happy hour–friendly at the same time. Start with an order of fried mushrooms or fried green tomatoes (or, if you need more fried temptations, the country platter, which comes with fried pickles, mushrooms, green tomatoes, and stuffed jalapeños). Then move on to menu items such as pulled pork quesadillas, the delicious honey jerk salmon salad, a perfectly cooked turkey burger, or even a classic chili cheese dog. No matter what you order, you won't go wrong here. Wash it down with one of the many Texas beers on tap (I like the Real Ale Rio Blanco Pale Ale) or a mixed drink.

Chatters Cafe and Bistro, 140 S. Heights Blvd., Houston, TX 77007; (713) 864-8080; www.chatterscafe.com; Breakfast; $$. This is one of my favorite brunch destinations in Houston thanks to its fantastic menu and servers who ensure that you rarely have to wait, even on a Sunday morning. The building is large—there's indoor and outdoor seating—and the menu is basic but dependable, ranging from omelets to French toast to smoked salmon Benedict. Don't forget to order a side of pancakes, either—they're delicious. Brunch is served on weekends from 10 a.m. to 3 p.m. Lunch and dinner include quesadillas, salads, burgers, wraps, pizza, and sandwiches. The prices here tend to be very reasonable, and the portion sizes are large—be sure to ask for a take-out box. There's also a full beer and wine menu and a great happy hour. A second location is at 1275 Eldridge Pkwy., Ste. 100.

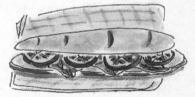

Christian's Tailgate Bar and Grill, 2000 Bagby St., Houston, TX 77002; (713) 527-0261; www.christianstailgate.com; American; $. I've had so many random experiences here. I've bested a stranger in an arm-wrestling competition; sung along during a heated karaoke contest; and watched nearly every type of sport you can imagine on the big-screen TV. But no matter what experience you have here, nothing will beat having lunch or dinner here. That's because this one-time dive is now serving up some of the best—and best-known—hamburgers in the state. Expect ⅓-, ½-, and 1-pound varieties served dry, with swiss cheese and mushrooms or open-faced and smothered in chili. Other add-ons include jalapeños, bacon, and onion rings. Other menu items are also available, including a Southwest Baja egg roll, jalapeño poppers, chips and salsa, taquitos, grilled chicken salad, and a variety of fabulous sandwiches including a steak sandwich (prime rib eye with swiss cheese, grilled onions, and mayo), a grilled cheese, a grilled chicken sandwich, and a BLT. Chicken tenders, hot dogs, seafood baskets, and a kids' menu are also available, as is a full beer list. Additional locations at 7340 Washington Ave and 2820 White Oak.

Cleburne Cafeteria, 3606 Bissonnet St., Houston, TX 77005; (713) 667-2386; www.cleburnecafeteria.com; Southern; $$. The best description I can give for Cleburne Cafeteria is Luby's meets Grandma's kitchen. This cafeteria-style restaurant is consistent with its Southern-style food and wonderful, homemade desserts. Think fried chicken, turkey and dressing, beef stew, chicken and dumplings, meat loaf, mashed potatoes, creamed spinach, mac

and cheese, etc. Prices can be a bit higher than you might expect, but all of the bakery items—pies, cakes, cobblers, puddings, and tarts—are made fresh daily and most ingredients come directly from a local farmers' market. You should know, however, that the cafeteria is closed on Saturday. Also, it can get packed on Sunday, so it's a good idea to get there early. Only cash and checks are accepted.

D'Amico's Italian Market Cafe, 5510 Morningside Dr., Houston, TX 77005; (713) 526-3400; www.damico-cafe.com; Italian; $$. Part cafe, part restaurant, D'Amico's Italian Market Cafe is a wonderful place to go when you're in the Rice Village area and want a quick lunch. You'll find a variety of Italian fare that includes small portions of lasagna, ravioli, and other pastas as well as salads, sandwiches, and pizza. At lunchtime, between 11 a.m. and 2 p.m., you can also sample three items for just $7.95. A full dinner menu is also served. The place can get busy, but if you can, grab a seat on the outside patio, which overlooks a bustling part of the outdoor shopping area and makes for great people watching. My favorite menu items here include Caprese salad, the tortellini Genovese (homemade spinach pasta stuffed with chicken and pancetta in Alfredo sauce with prosciutto and green peas), and rolled stuffed eggplant. There's also a fantastic (though small) on-site Italian deli selling items such as meats, pasta, canned goods, and pastries.

Danton's Gulf Coast Seafood Kitchen, 4611 Montrose Blvd., Houston, TX 77006; (713) 807-8883; www.dantonsseafood.com; Seafood; $$$. This restaurant, one of the newer in Houston, is operated by lifelong friends—and it shows in the hospitality you feel when you walk through the door. Specializing in Gulf Coast seafood dishes, Danton's has a cool, 1920s feel, actual sketches of the coast by artist Richard Fowles, and delicious, super-fresh seafood. Menu favorites include the baked oysters Dan (fresh shucked oysters with garlic butter, jumbo lump crabmeat, bread crumbs, Parmesan cheese, and Dan's spice); crab bisque loaded with blue crab claw meat; the T-Wayne Boy (grilled onion pork sausage served on french bread with mayo, Creole mustard, and red onion); baked crab Balinese with jumbo lump crab, bell peppers, onions, and Dan's spice, topped with Parmesan cheese and baked; and flounder with crab-cake stuffing. There's also a wonderful brunch on Sunday that features local blues artists and seafood-inspired brunch dishes, such as snapper meunière, *migas,* duck and andouille gumbo, and eggs Benedict Danton. Brunch runs from 11 a.m. to 4 p.m.

Del Frisco's Double Eagle Steakhouse, 5061 Westheimer Rd., Houston, TX 77056; (713) 355-2600; www.delfriscos.com; Steak House; $$$. One of just a handful of Del Frisco's restaurants in the country, Houston's Del Frisco's Double Eagle Steakhouse serves up delightful upscale dishes in a classy, romantic atmosphere—this is a prime spot for a date night or anniversary dinner. Some of the meats look wonderful, but I've never gone wrong with the seafood offerings, so that's what I end up sticking with. Start with the crab cakes, wedge salad, or ahi tuna tartare, followed by sesame seared tuna or sautéed salmon with a side of jalapeño mac and cheese. Top it all off with some bread pudding or chocolate lava cake. This place is particularly good about holidays—think handwritten notes and free glasses of bubbly—so I recommend it for special occasions.

Down House, 1801 Yale St., Houston, TX 77008; (713) 864-3696; www.downhousehouston.com; American; $$. This restaurant burst onto the culinary scene last summer and was an almost instant hit. Open for breakfast, lunch, and evening bites, Down House prides itself on buying locally from providers such as Sabra Ranch, Broken Arrow Ranch, Dustin Hoeinghaus Eggs, Buddy's Chicken, Black Hill Ranch, and Slow Dough Baking Co. What does that mean? Fare tastes incredibly fresh and, well, delicious. Breakfast offerings range from standards such as steel-cut oatmeal, whole-grain waffles, and breakfast tacos (black beans, *queso fresco,* avocado, and pico de gallo, for example) to innovative items, such as a breakfast *torta* with pulled pork, avocado, coleslaw, and a fried local egg on a fresh *bolillo.* In terms of lunch, you've got your choice of fresh salads and about a half dozen sandwiches, such as the free-range lemon chicken (with olive tapenade, feta cream, and sautéed spinach on a challah roll) or the longhorn burger (with Texas gold cheddar, arugula, tomato, and house-made mustard or aioli). Finish up your meal with a scoop of sorbet or gelato, or a house-baked chocolate chip pecan cookie.

El Meson Cuban Restaurant, 2425 University Blvd., Houston, TX 77005; (713) 522-9306; www.elmeson.com; Cuban; $$$. I love coming to this place for its special events, particularly its Spanish wine dinners featuring classical wines from Spain paired with traditional dishes such as codfish baked with toasted garlic and parsley, serrano ham croquettes with oyster mushroom, roasted domestic leg of lamb with braised potatoes and Riojano sausage, and pound cake with cabrales cheese. No matter when you come, however, you can expect delicious paella made with Spanish saffron mixed with items such as prawns, shrimp, squid, mussels, chicken, chorizo, salmon, duck, lamb, pork tenderloin, and more. Other menu items include gazpacho, enchiladas, *carne guisada,* nachos, quesadillas, and tapas such as serrano ham with Manchego cheese, Spanish potato omelets, and spicy braised potatoes in tomato sauce. The restaurant, which is located in Rice Village, is open from 11 a.m. to 10 p.m. Mon through Thurs, 11 a.m. to 11 p.m. Fri, 11 a.m. to 10 p.m. Sat, and noon to 10 p.m. Sun.

El Tiempo Cantina, 5602 Washington Ave., Houston, TX 77007; (713) 807-1600; www.eltiempocantina.com; Tex-Mex; $$$. Houston has its share of Tex-Mex restaurants, and trust me when I say many of them are not worth mentioning. El Tiempo, however, quickly became a favorite of mine thanks to its sprawling patio, perfectly crafted margaritas, and excellent food. Menu favorites here include the beef tenderloin and chicken fajitas, enchiladas, deep-fried peppers stuffed with shrimp and cheese, crab nachos, and chicken soup. Not feeling very hungry? Order a side of tortillas and dip them into the perfectly made warm salsa. It's a little slice of heaven. The menu items here are a little pricier than at most Tex-Mex joints, but worth it. A second location is at 3130 Richmond Ave.

Empire Cafe, 1732 Westheimer Rd., Houston, TX 77019; (713) 528-5282; www.empirecafe.com; Breakfast; $$. I initially became a fan of this place because of its incredible cakes, such as chocolate Italian cream, carrot, lemon poppy seed, Toll House, and Chocolate Blackout—all of which are half price on Monday. But this is also a wonderful place to go for a meal, particularly breakfast. Breakfast selections include a gingerbread waffle, focaccia bread topped with scrambled eggs, breakfast tacos, omelets, and frittatas. The restaurant is also open for lunch and dinner, when it serves up incredible paninis (try the roasted eggplant with caramelized onions, mixed greens, and basil pecan pesto), pizzas, soups, salads, pastas, and more. There's also a full coffee bar as well as a selection of beer and wine.

Feast, 219 Westheimer Rd., Houston, TX 77006; (713) 529-7788; www.feasthouston.com; British; $$$. Regardless of whether it succeeded, this restaurant was bound to make a splash thanks to its head-to-tail philosophy, as in every part of the animal is used to make innovative (and usually wonderful) dishes. Included among them: calf's liver and bacon with bubble and squeak, spinach, and onion gravy; pork cheeks with red peppers and Rioja; and braised lamb necks with red beans and mustard greens. Prefer something more traditional? The menu has you covered there, with excellent selections including braised lamb shank, garlic snails on toast, ratatouille-stuffed giant squash with herbed couscous, Scottish smoked salmon, and chicken and mushroom pie with swiss chard. Want to know exactly where your dinner came from? Feast keeps an updated list of the local farms that provide its animals, dairy products, eggs, bacon, and more. Any foodie living in or visiting Houston absolutely must make a trip to Feast.

Field of Greens, 2320 W. Alabama St., Houston, TX 77098; (713) 533-0029; www.fieldofgreenscuisine.com; Vegetarian; $$. The atmosphere at this restaurant, located in a strip mall, is lackluster, but if you're looking for unique vegetarian and vegan cuisine, this is still a great place to try. Specializing in everything from raw and macrobiotic fare to cheese-topped specialties, Field of Greens is one of the few places in Houston that is completely vegan friendly.

Favorite menu options here include the Eden burger, a barbecue soy patty with shiitake mushrooms, lettuce, tomato, sprouts, crispy basil bean curd, and mayo; the vegan macrobiotic platter with a steamed vegetable medley, kale with miso sauce, organic brown rice, daily beans, tofu quiche, pickled daikon, and seaweed served with a cup of miso soup; the vegan lasagna, made with roasted zucchini, squash, mushrooms, spinach, vegan mozzarella, and marinara, served with a side salad; and the vegan green bean hummus wrap with fried green beans, grilled soy ham, and hummus wrapped in a whole-wheat tortilla and served with a side salad. When you're finished, head next door to check out the Path of Tea tearoom.

Glass Wall, 933 Studewood St., Houston, TX 77008; (713) 868-7930; www.glasswalltherestaurant.com; American; $$$. One of the first nice restaurants in the Heights area, the Glass Wall has grown from an area favorite to a city destination, with upscale bistro fare that will impress even the most jaded foodie. Start with the perfectly cooked Chesapeake crab cake with mango aioli and mango jicama slaw or the local tomato salad with red onion, basil, fresh mozzarella, and balsamic syrup. Then move on to a main course of potato-chip chicken-fried steak with jalapeño cream gravy and horseradish smashers; Hereford rib eye with red pesto smashers, sautéed foraged mushrooms, and maître d'hotel butter and Cabernet jus; or, my favorite, the boudin-stuffed Texas quail with Creole fried rice, fried okra, and gumbo jus. Not sure what wine to order? Entree and wine pairings are suggested on the menu. Sunday brunch is also available.

Goode's Armadillo Palace, 5015 Kirby Dr., Houston, TX 77098; (713) 526-9700; www.goodecompany.com; Barbecue; $$. Just look for the giant glittering armadillo out front and you'll know you're at the right place. Part honky-tonk, part barbecue joint, Goode's

Armadillo Palace is a must-visit restaurant in Houston. Part of the legendary Goode Company chain, Goode's Armadillo Palace serves up a variety of Texas and Tex-Mex favorites as well as regular live music in a really fun atmosphere. Among my favorite menu items: chicken and cheese flautas with avocado cream sauce; the Gulf shrimp remoulade salad with fresh avocado, croutons, Gulf shrimp, remoulade sauce, and Parmesan cheese; old-fashioned Frito pie with venison chili, Fritos, grated cheddar, and diced onions; and the Peace Maker sandwich with New York strip steak, melted white cheddar, Shiner Bock–braised onions, and horseradish sauce on a bun, served with fries.

Gravitas, 807 Taft St., Houston, TX 77019; (713) 522-0995; www.gravitasrestaurant.com; American; $$$. Owned by Scott Tycer, one of Houston's most renowned chefs, Gravitas offers American bistro-style cuisine from a menu filled with delicious, food-forward offerings. Among them: crispy pork with Thai salad and kimchee dressing; pierogies with brown butter and bacon; Atlantic salmon with spinach puree, salsify, and beurre blanc; a smothered pork chop with three-onion bread pudding and artichokes; and beef bourguignon with potato puree, mushrooms, and asparagus. And don't miss the daily specials, which include dishes such as stuffed trout, roasted half duck, and roasted whole fish. Brunch, lunch, and happy hour are also offered.

The Grove, 1611 Lamar St., Houston, TX 77010; (713) 337-7314; www.thegrovehouston.com; American; $$$. In an effort to green-ify Houston and give residents and visitors a reason to visit downtown on the weekends, the city poured millions of dollars into Discovery Green, a multiuse urban park that offers farmers' markets, free movies, workout classes, and concerts. Anchoring one end of the now popular space is The Grove, a casual, eco-friendly eatery located in a 10,000-square-foot space constructed of glass, wood, and steel that features casual American food as well as an on-site herb and tomato garden and tree house deck. The menu at the restaurant, run by the Schiller Del Grande Restaurant Group, includes items such as pork belly sliders, sautéed baby artichokes, brick pressed Cornish hen, wood-grilled marinated vegetable skewers, Hill Country venison, and a grilled shrimp burger.

Haven, 2502 Algerian Way, Houston, TX 77098; (713) 581-6101; www.havenhouston.com; Southern; $$$. This restaurant by Chef Randy Evans has dubbed itself a "seasonal kitchen," meaning it serves only seasonal, local ingredients. The payoff for you? Food that tastes super fresh. Main dishes include free-range chicken with bacon spaetzle and crispy brussels sprouts; quail with jalapeño sausage dressing and green tomato golden raisin chutney; and peanut crusted soft-shell crab with spring veggie sauté and *nuoc mam*. I'm also a huge fan of the restaurant's fun appetizers, such as free-range deviled eggs, crispy pig-trotter fritters, shrimp corn dogs, and a relish

A Food Lovers' Guide to Tex-Mex

If you're eating Tex-Mex or Mexican food for the first time, you may see some unfamiliar items on the menu. Here's a glossary of some names you're likely to see:

Antojitos: Appetizers or tapas

Botanas: Appetizers

Breakfast taco: Eggs, cheese, and sometimes meat, peppers, or potatoes wrapped in a tortilla; topped with salsa

Cabrito: Young goat, typically very tender

Camarones: Shrimp

Cerveza: Beer

Chalupa: Flat, crispy shell topped with chicken, pork, lettuce, tomatoes, cheese, and/or salsa

Chilaquiles: Fried corn tortillas topped with salsa or mole, cheese, and scrambled or fried eggs

Chile rellenos: Stuffed peppers

Chili *con carne:* Chili with meat

Chorizo: Spicy pork sausage

Codorniz a las Brazas: Grilled quail

Costillas de Cerdo al Carbon: Pork ribs

Empanadas: Pastry stuffed with ground-up vegetables and meats

Enchilada: Tortilla wrapped around a hot filling, such as cheese, beef, spinach, or chicken lathered with a sauce

Ensalada: Salad

Fajitas: Grilled strips of steak or chicken eaten in a flour tortilla; usually served with pico de gallo, cheese, and sour cream on the side

Frijoles refritos: Refried beans

Guacamole: Chopped avocado dip peppered with herbs, chopped onions, and chiles

Huevos rancheros: Fried eggs with a tomato-chile sauce

Margarita: Mixed drink made with tequila and lime, served in a salted glass; sometimes includes other flavors such as mango or strawberry

Migas: Eggs scrambled with cheese and corn tortilla strips or chips

Mole: Sauce made of unsweetened chocolate, nuts, and spices; served on top of enchiladas

Mollejas al Ajillo: Sautéed sweetbreads with garlic, Guajillo, and olive oil; typically served with tortillas to make tacos

Pico de gallo: Spicy salsa made with tomatoes, onions, chiles, and cilantro

Quesadilla: Two tortillas with cheese between them, served baked

Queso: Cheese dip, often made with Mexican cheese; sometimes includes peppers

Queso con carne: Cheese dip with meat

Salsa *verde:* Green salsa made with green chiles, garlic, cilantro, and tomatillos; often used on top of enchiladas or for dipping tortilla chips

Sopapilla: Fried pastry topped with honey

Tamale: Corn dough filled with pork, chicken, or vegetables and rolled in a corn husk; served steamed, sometimes with a chile sauce

Tortilla: A flat round bread, usually made of corn, flour, or whole wheat; used to make enchiladas and to accompany dishes such as fajitas and *migas*

Tostada: Fried tortilla

tray with pickled vegetables, pimento cheese–stuffed celery, and marinated olives. Brunch and lunch are also offered. Cocktails here include a variety of classics such as the Tom Collins, a Pisco Sour, a Manhattan, and an Old-fashioned Rum Cocktail.

Hobbit Cafe, 2243 Richmond Ave., Houston, TX 77098; (713) 526-5460; www.myhobbitcafe.com; Vegetarian; $$. Hobbit Cafe has long been a favorite among Houston's vegetarians because of its wide variety of non-meat and even vegan items. But if you're a carnivore, never fear—there's plenty for you here as well. The food is high-quality yet unfussy, and the portion sizes are generous. Menu standouts include the "hobbit-made" black bean burger served with kettle-cooked potato chips; the zucchini and eggplant enchiladas with roasted tomato pepper sauce and cheddar cheese served with brown rice, black beans, and pico de gallo; and the Hobbit Wrap, with mixed greens, tomato, red onion, cucumber, feta cheese, and Caesar dressing in a large tomato basil wrap. Many menu items can be made vegan. Be warned: The building is small, so you might have a slight wait. And yes, in case you're wondering, the restaurant is decorated in *Lord of the Rings* paraphernalia, so if you're a fan, it's definitely a must-see.

House of Pies, 3112 Kirby Dr., Houston, TX 77098; (713) 528-3816; www.houseofpies.com; 24-Hour Dining; $$. This place is legendary in Houston, not just for its fantastic selection of pies (we'll get to that in a minute) and the fact that it's open 24 hours a day, but also for its breakfast, lunch, and dinner fare. Offerings in the a.m. are standard but well prepared and include corned beef hash and eggs; a country breakfast with pancakes, eggs, bacon, and sausage; and fruit-infused pancakes and waffles. Other items are also predictable but perfectly seasoned, including a wonderful array of sandwiches (chicken-fried

steak sandwich, Monte Cristo, and turkey, bacon, and swiss melt) at lunch and Southern skillet fare at dinner, such as Olde English fish and chips, a rib eye steak dinner, and grilled chicken breast topped with mushrooms. Now let's talk about the pies. Every day expect dozens of varieties that include pumpkin, fresh strawberry, Texas pecan, wild blueberry, banana cream, lemon meringue, German chocolate cream, and, my absolute favorite, Bayou Goo, a pecan crust with a layer of sweet cream cheese, vanilla custard, and chocolate chunks topped with whipped cream and chocolate shavings. If you go late at night on a weekend, expect the crowd to be, er, unreliable (read: drunk), but the service and food are always a hit. A second location is at 6142 Westheimer Rd.

Hubcap Grill, 1111 Prairie St., Houston, TX 77002; (713) 223-5885; www.hubcapgrill.com; Barbecue; $. This hole-in-the-wall located downtown near Minute Maid Park has been many things over the years, but when Hubcap Grill opened there, Houstonians quickly realized something special was happening. Open only from 11 a.m. to 3 p.m. Mon through Sat for lunch, Hubcap Grill offers

up what are arguably the best burgers in the city: fresh-ground patties on homemade, toasted buns served with fresh-cut fries. Options here include the Triple Heart Clogger (fresh ground patty with a grilled "wiener," bacon, and cheese), the Hubcap Decker (2 patties layered with toasted buns and American and swiss cheese, and topped with lettuce, tomatoes, pickles, and onions), and the Sticky Burger (patty, peanut butter—yes, really—bacon, and American cheese). Not into red meat? Hubcap also serves a variety of chicken sandwiches. A second location is at 1133 W. 19th St.

Huynh Restaurant, 912 St. Emanuel St., Houston, TX 77003; (713) 224-8964; http://huynhrestauranthouston.com; Vietnamese; $. Houston is fortunate to have a number of truly standout Vietnamese restaurants, and Huynh is one of my favorites for a number of reasons. First, it's located in the up-and-coming EaDo district, also a good place to catch a concert or grab a beer without having to worry too much about finding parking. The restaurant itself is sleek and modern, but the food tastes like something that came out of Grandma's kitchen: satisfying, nourishing, and delicious, all at once. Menu favorites include pulled duck meat with fresh herbs and vegetables, served with ginger dipping sauce; crispy Vietnamese egg rolls served with fresh herbs and lettuce for wrapping; stir-fried beef tenderloin with peppers and onions; *pho* served with a variety of meats; and fish soup with pork, shrimp, vegetables, and wide rice noodles. Hit the liquor store before you come—it's BYOB. Open daily except Sunday.

Ibiza Food and Wine Bar, 2450 Louisiana St., Ste. 200, Houston, TX 77006; (713) 524-0004; www.ibizafoodandwinebar.com; Spanish; $$$. This Spanish-inspired restaurant can get pricey, particularly if you're going to be drinking wine. But don't let that keep you from coming here. From incredible lobster risotto to a chocolate bread pudding that will change your life, Ibiza's delicious food and classy atmosphere make it a standout in Houston's food scene. Start with a sampling of small plates (think tapas), such as Spanish white anchovies with parsley and lemon; local goat cheese with Morcilla sausage and sweet roasted beets; or a crispy long-stem artichoke with Meyer lemon aioli. Then move on to a main course that could include 6-hour braised lamb shank with Spanish mint oil; Colorado ruby red trout with salsa verde; slow-roasted salmon with tomato and sweet corn; and Catalan meatballs and roasted peppers with chipotle mashed potatoes.

Indika, 516 Westheimer Rd., Houston, TX 77006; (713) 524-2170; www.indikausa.com; Indian; $$$. With a goal of offering progressive Indian fare using fresh, local ingredients, Chef Anita Jaisinghani has achieved success in creating one of the most innovative Indian restaurants in the city. Examples of this fusion cuisine can be seen throughout the menu, which includes dishes such as grilled Texas red snapper with spinach, fenugreek, and almond curry; roasted poblano stuffed with a slow-cooked pork masala, beets, and lentil curry; and coriander and black pepper–crusted venison chops with wild mushrooms slow cooked in Old Monk rum. And don't miss the starters, particularly the warm spinach and *paneer* tandoori corn roti or the kale and blueberry salad. The restaurant also offers daily lunch, Sunday brunch, and hands-on cooking classes on the fourth Sunday of every month. Register in advance.

Irma's Houston, 22 N. Chenevert St., Houston, TX 77002; (713) 222-0767; http://irmashouston.com; Tex-Mex; $$. Many a hungry Houstonian has stumbled upon this top-notch joint on the way to an Astros game (after all, it's just down the street from Minute Maid Park), and generally one visit is all it takes to get hooked on the quality Tex-Mex fare coming from the kitchen. Expect new items every day—as in, there's no set menu except for the more than a dozen specials offered each day—and even an occasional celebrity sighting: Many of Houston's well-known residents, including rapper Paul Wall, consider Irma's among their favorite places to eat. Menu items rotate but include dishes such as fish tacos, chile rellenos, enchiladas, soft tacos, and out-of-this-world lemonade.

James Coney Island, 3607 S. Shepherd Dr., Houston, TX 77098; (713) 524-7400; www.jamesconeyisland.com; American; $. With nearly two dozen stores in the Houston area, James Coney Island is the go-to place when you're craving a quick frank. But what many people don't realize about James Coney Island, which has been serving Coney-style dogs since 1923, is that the food here is really, really good. The buns are baked fresh and cut in a way that keeps all the toppings nestled in close to the hot dog. Hot dog varieties include Texas style (mustard, chili, cheese, and onion),

Chicago style (mustard, relish, onions, pickle spear, sport peppers, and celery salt), New York style (regular or jumbo dog with mustard, chili, cheese, and onion), a jalapeño dog, a turkey dog, and the original (mustard, chili sauce, and onions). The restaurant also recently revamped its menus to offer specialty items such as premium burgers and Greek salad. Specials such as kids eat free every Wednesday from 4 p.m. to close and 99-cent original Coneys on Sunday offer an added incentive to come by. Want something on the side? French fries, tater tots, onion rings, tamales, chips, and "world famous" chili are also available. Check website for additional locations.

Jenni's Noodle House, 602 E. 20th St., Houston, TX 77008; (713) 862-3344; www.noodlesrule.com; Vietnamese; $$. The motto here is "It's all good in the Noodlehood," and that's a more than apt description of this wonderful local Vietnamese joint. Specializing in noodles of all types, from vermicelli salads to *pho* (traditional Vietnamese beef noodle soup) to Art Car curry (with potatoes, mushrooms, carrots, tofu and jasmine rice), this is the perfect place to get your noodle fix. Other popular menu items include the Vietnamese egg rolls, steamed edamame, dream rolls (rice paper, tofu, shiitake, lettuce, mint, and vermicelli), seaweed salad, wonton soup, and salt-'n'-pepper shrimp. Other locations can be found at 3111 S. Shepherd Dr. and 2027 Post Oak Blvd.

Katz's Deli and Bar, 616 Westheimer Rd., Houston, TX 77006; (713) 521-3838; www.ilovekatzs.com; 24-Hour Dining; $$. The motto at this chain deli and bar is "Katz's never kloses," and that pretty much sums it up. With a 24-hour menu that includes a full range of items, from breakfast to dinner to scrumptious desserts, this place is a hit—any time of day. One of the best places to start, particularly if you're hungry, is the sandwich selection, which is a meat lover's dream. The half-pound sandwich menu includes varieties such as corned beef brisket, hot pastrami, fresh home-made chopped chicken liver, farm fresh egg salad, Hebrew National salami, and beef tongue. Other menu favorites include French onion soup, fried pickles, mac and cheese, and matzo ball soup. Desserts include the "world's tallest 7-layer cake," caramel fudge cheese-cake, macaroons, and a cheesecake shake made with a whole slice of cheesecake blended with vanilla, chocolate, or strawberry flavorings. Oh, and the people watching here is fabulous.

Khun Kay Thai, 1209 Montrose Blvd., Houston, TX 77019; (713) 524-9614; www.khunkaythaicafe.com; Thai; $$. Located in the heart of Montrose, Khun Kay Thai offers a delicious selection of Thai dishes, many of which incorporate true Texas elements. Among those options: the jalapeño mixed stir-fry with onions, jalapeño peppers, and green beans; basil eggplant with brown sauce and basil; Thai tacos with fresh tofu in a spicy lime sauce, served with fresh ginger, roasted peanuts, and a lettuce or cabbage "taco shell"; and stir-fried tofu with flat rice noodles and fresh vegetables. A full menu of meat dishes is also available. Some of my favorite dishes here have included the *tom yum* soup (Thailand's national soup, with lemon-lime juice, lemongrass, Kaffir lime leaf, and mushrooms in hot and sour soup), the garlic wok stir-fry, and the perfectly cooked pad thai with chicken. The place is technically a sit-down restaurant, although it doesn't have much atmosphere, so it's just as good to grab something to go. And if you want it spicy, they will make it spicy. Open daily for lunch and dinner.

Khyber North Indian Grill, 2510 Richmond Ave., Houston, TX 77098; (713) 942-9424; Indian; $$. Khyber is partially known for its funny, ever-changing sign in front of the building, but even more so it's known for its delicious Indian fare. This was one of the first Indian restaurants I tried when I moved to Houston nearly a decade ago, and it remains one of my favorite places when I need an Indian food fix. Standout dishes include the chicken tikka masala, *saag paneer*, lamb curry, chicken vindaloo, and chicken korma. And be sure to start with an order of samosas and some naan. Many options are available here for both vegetarians and non-vegetarians.

La Griglia, 2002 W. Gray, Houston, TX 77019; (713) 526-4700; www.lagrigliarestaurant.com; Italian; $$$. If you want to rub elbows with Houston's rich and famous, this is the place to come. The atmosphere, which incorporates Italian murals and bright, festive tiling, is inviting yet intimate and the staff is welcoming yet professional. But the Italian-inspired food here is the real draw. Try a starter such as shrimp and crab cheesecake (blue crab and Gulf shrimp baked in mascarpone custard) or crab claws sautéed in Chianti, garlic, San Marzano tomatoes, herbs, and crushed red pepper. Then follow it up with one of a dozen entree salads (the La Griglia chopped salad, with roasted chicken, provolone, applewood-smoked bacon, and tomato vinaigrette, is my favorite), an order of house-made ribbon pasta tossed in beef, veal, or pork ragout, or open-flame rotisserie chicken.

Lankford Market, 88 Dennis St., Houston, TX 77006; (713) 522-9555; http://lankfordgrocery.com; Southern; $$. One of my favorite Houston institutions, this quaint little grocery store/dive looks unassuming from the outside. But once you walk in, you instantly realize that this place takes food seriously. It's best known for its selection of burgers—which were featured on the Food Network's *Diners, Drive-Ins, and Dives*—that includes old-fashioned, double-meat, triple-meat, the Grim Burger (mac and cheese, bacon, fried egg, and jalapeño), and the South of the Border (Monterey Jack, pico de gallo, avocado, and cilantro dressing).  Most burgers cost around $6. The mission state-ment here reads, "We have nothing small, nothing healthy, and nothing fast." Other menu items include a chicken strip sandwich, chicken sliders, a BLT sandwich, and a tuna melt. Breakfast is also offered Mon though Sat. Don't miss the daily specials, either, which include the incredible enchilada dinner on Wednesday and the perfectly prepared chicken-fried steak on Thursday.

Les Givral's Kahve, 801 Congress St., Houston, TX 77002; (713) 547-0444; www.lesgivrals.com; Vietnamese; $. Despite considering myself a longtime foodie, I'll admit to not having my first Vietnamese sandwich until I moved to Houston eight years ago. The first place I had one? Les Givral's. One bite into the crusty, fresh-baked roll stuffed with perfectly cooked tofu and spice-charged with a hidden jalapeño and I was hooked. But there's more to Les Givral's Kahve than just its sandwiches. You'll also find rice-noodle soups filled with everything from meatballs to round eye steak to chicken, fried rice, and incredible spring rolls. The Congress location is closed on weekends; a second location at 4601 Washington Ave. is open daily.

Little Bigs, 2703 Montrose Blvd., Houston, TX 77006; (713) 521-2447; www.littlebigshouston.com; American; $$. Brian Caswell has been Houston's golden boy for quite a while now, as every restaurant he touches, from the famous **Reef** (see p. 51) to the newish **El Real,** seems to turn to gold. But when he opened up this burger joint in the heart of the Montrose district, he was not without critics who wondered how his upscale approach to cuisine would translate. Fortunately, there was no need to worry. Little Bigs has managed to serve up some of the best burgers in Houston, namely a signature 3-ounce all-beef slider served on bread plucked from the oven every 3 hours. There's also a breaded chicken breast slider, a vegetarian black bean slider, and a Carolina-style pulled pork slider. Don't miss the hand-cut French fries, hand-dipped shakes, and impressive selection of beer and wine.

Mardi Gras Grill, 1200 Durham Dr., Houston, TX 77007; (713) 864-5600; www.mardigrasgrill.net; Cajun; $$. Crawfish season is a fabulous time in Houston, when locals of all shapes and sizes unite to don bibs and nosh on messy but oh-so-delicious mudbugs until they're ready to burst. Mardi Gras Grill is among the best places in town for a crawfish fix, but even if it's not crawfish season, you should still visit this wonderful little restaurant, with one of the greatest selections of casual Cajun fare around. Don't miss the incredible boudin balls, chicken and sausage gumbo, fried-oyster po'boys, jambalaya, crawfish étouffée, and blackened chicken with shrimp. All meals come with fresh buttered bread. Oh, the hurricanes here are pretty mighty as well. Grab a spot on the wide outside deck and get ready to let the good times roll.

Mark's American Cuisine, 1658 Westheimer Rd., Houston, TX 77006; (713) 523-3800; www.marks1658.com; American; $$$$. A front-runner for Houston's favorite upscale restaurant, Mark's American Cuisine serves up progressive American cuisine inside a gorgeous 1920s church. Think candlelit tables, golden ceilings, and hand-painted Art Deco walls—no wonder it's considered one of Houston's most romantic places to eat. On the menu, expect delights from chef Mark Cox, who offers lunch Monday through

Friday and dinner daily. Four menus are offered on a regular basis: a seasonal menu; a "recommended menu" of the chef's personal choices (changes twice a day); a verbal menu that highlights items that have just arrived; and a create-your-own-dinner menu that allows you to piece together the dishes you'd like. Expect appetizers such as *foie gras* and quail and turtle soup, and entrees such as grilled Scottish salmon with coconut risotto, a maple sugar, ginger, and coffee-roasted pork loin with bourbon short ribs, and prime sirloin with chicken-fried bacon. The wine list is also extensive.

Max's Wine Dive, 4720 Washington Ave., Houston, TX 77007; (713) 880-8737; www.maxswinedive.com; Southern; $$. Max's Wine Dive has expanded to include locations in San Antonio and Austin, but I still like the original location on Washington Avenue the best. Offering upscale comfort food in a casual atmosphere ("Fried chicken and Champagne? Why the hell not?" is among the mottos here), Max's Wine Dive is a Houston favorite for innovative, interesting fare. Among the menu items here: gator beignets with jalapeño aioli; a fried egg sandwich with truffle oil, applewood-smoked bacon, and gruyère; a Texas "haute" dog served on a Slow Dough Bread Co. baguette; and a house-made sausage and pretzel burger with crawfish boil potato salad. And true to the name, many, many wines are available here by the bottle or the glass. Sunday brunch and Friday lunch are also served.

Mi Luna Tapas Restaurant and Bar, 2441 University Blvd., Houston, TX 77005; (713) 520-5025; www.mi-luna.net; Tapas; $$. For starters, you should know that Mi Luna serves up some of the best frozen margaritas in the city—seriously, I've had a difficult time finding any I like better. You should also know that on certain nights the restaurant features live music that may have you wanting to get up and dance—particularly after a few drinks. And finally, they have really great tapas that always manage to quell my urge to visit Barcelona again—at least for a day or two. The list of tapas—both cold and hot—here is impressive, ranging from simple dishes such as cheese plates and marinated olives to more complicated and flavorful fare such as quail and figs with chipotle chocolate glaze, grilled squid with roasted garlic vinaigrette on a bed of fresh spinach, pan-seared monkfish and toasted almonds and honey saffron cream sauce, and braised veal tongue in walnut port wine sauce. They also have a variety of Spanish classics, such as *patatas bravas* (sautéed potatoes in a spicy tomato sauce), *pinchos de carne* (grilled, skewered beef tenderloin with saffron rice and caramelized onions), and tortilla a la Espanola (Spanish potato omelet with onions).

Mockingbird Bistro, 1985 Welch St., Houston, TX 77019; (713) 533-0200; www.mockingbirdbistro.com; French; $$$. It's hard to believe that Mockingbird Bistro, run by Chef-Owner John Sheely, has been open for almost a decade—its service and fare have become so dependably good that sometimes you almost forget it's still there.

But make a point not to forget about Mockingbird Bistro, because you're likely to have one of the best meals you've had in months each time you come here. Known for Texas-meets-France cuisine, the fare at Mockingbird Bistro includes veal sweetbreads with spring onions, mushrooms, and tarragon cream sauce; Washington state black mussels with tomato, garlic, red curry, coconut milk, and garlic toast; chilled tomato melon gazpacho with grilled shrimp and garlic crostini; strawberry grouper with crawfish, *haricots verts,* oyster mushrooms, and horseradish beurre noisette; Kurobuta pork chop with ragout of baby cabbage and mushrooms with whipped potatoes and a red wine reduction; and strip loin steak frites, with caramelized shallots, arugula, and *pommes frites.* Brunch, lunch, happy hour, and monthly wine dinners are also offered.

Molina's Cantina, 4720 Washington Ave., Houston, TX 77007; (713) 862-0013; www.molinasrestaurants.com; Tex-Mex; $$. With so many choices along the bustling Washington Avenue restaurant corridor, it can be difficult to decide where to eat. Even if you have a hankering for Tex-Mex specifically, you have a number of options to choose from. I frequently find myself heading to Molina's, however, for the flavorful, excellent margaritas and perfectly prepared Tex-Mex fare. The first thing you need to do when you sit down is place an order for Jose's Dip, a fabulous concoction of *queso* blended with taco meat that is a specialty here. In terms of entrees, you can't go wrong with the tamales, enchiladas, or tacos *al carbon,* but I recommend getting a combo platter, where you can sample several items all at once. The restaurant usually isn't too packed, which is another benefit to eating here. Try to get a spot on the patio if it's a nice night. An additional location is at 7901 Westheimer Rd. For Molina's Cantina's recipe for **Creamy Sopa De Poblana,** see p. 187.

Monarch Restaurant and Lounge, 5701 Main St. at Hotel ZaZa, Houston, TX 77005; (713) 527-1800; www.hotelzazahouston.com; American; $$. The first thing we need to talk about when discussing the Monarch Restaurant and Lounge at Hotel ZaZa is Sunday School. That's the playful name Monarch has given its Sunday brunch, which includes inventive cocktails such as the Bubble Berry (Bacardi dragon berry with Champagne and fresh berries); morning traditions such as lobster Benedict and an almond waffle with sliced almonds and chocolate butter; sharable dishes such as a deconstructed ahi roll and smoked salmon on mini crepes; and entrees such as ginger beef tenderloin, grilled salmon and scallops, and steak and eggs. Dessert options include cupcakes, white chocolate torte, and cheesecakes. There are also wonderful daily breakfast, lunch, and dinner menus, as well as a menu for the bikini-clad set headed out to the adjacent swimming pool. Other special events, such as half-price wine night on Monday and a summer wine tasting series, are also offered. For Monarch Restaurant and Lounge's recipe for the **Big Flirt,** see p. 205.

Mo's . . . A Place for Steaks, 1801 Post Oak Blvd., Houston, TX 77056; (713) 877-0720; www.mosaplaceforsteaks.com/houston; Steak House; $$$. With a sexy indoor atmosphere and a lovely outside patio that's perfect for sipping a cocktail any time of year, it's no wonder that Mo's . . . A Place for Steaks is among the favorite sip-and-sup spots for Houston celebrities. This is a true steak house, with options ranging from a horseradish-crusted rib eye to a certified Angus beef bone-in filet to a dry-aged bone-in New York strip, as well as other cuts in choose-your-own sizes. Not into steak? Don't worry—there's plenty more to whet your appetite. Consider the blue cheese and Dijon–crusted braised beef short ribs, the maple-planked salmon fillet, or the Australian lobster tail. And don't miss the incredible desserts, particularly the Mo cookie, a giant, half-baked chocolate chip cookie oozing with chocolate chips and topped with a heaping scoop of ice cream.

Oceanaire Seafood Room, 5061 Westheimer Rd., Houston, TX 77056; (832) 487-8862; www.theoceanaire.com; Seafood; $$$. If you've shopped at the Galleria, you probably know most of its restaurant offerings: the **Cheesecake Factory, Rainforest Cafe,** etc. But if you want something truly unique, pop by Oceanaire Seafood Room, a stunning seafood restaurant located right inside. Part of a national chain operated by Houston-based Landry's, Oceanaire Seafood Room serves up a variety of greatest-hits specialties and new classics in a lovely setting—expect giant aquariums that will impress both young and old. Start with one of my favorite appetizers: the Grilled Shrimp Diablo, which is wrapped in bacon with cream cheese and a jalapeño; the jumbo lump crab cake with creamy mustard mayo; or the escargots bourguignon with Burgundy butter and puff pastry. Then, move on to a main course of cioppino (San Francisco fisherman's stew), wild Alaskan halibut "cheeks" with citrus brown butter risotto and fried capers, or seared Copper River sockeye salmon with a sweet rice cake, cucumber salad, and miso butter sauce. Oceanaire is somewhat pricey, which is expected for this level of service and quality.

One's a Meal Greek Village, 812 Westheimer Rd., Houston, TX 77006; (713) 523-0425; www.onesameal.com; 24-Hour Dining; $$. We Houstonians are lucky to have a multitude of fantastic Greek restaurants in town, but when your hankering comes on late at night, there's only one place to turn: One's a Meal Greek Village. By serving up well-prepared Greek standards 24 hours a day, One's a Meal has established itself as a great place to go Greek—any time of day. The restaurant also serves up plain ol' American fare, meaning the menu is quite diverse, featuring items such as chicken kebab, dolmades, and spanakopita, as well as chicken tenders, spaghetti, and fried shrimp. Don't miss the wonderful calzones (I like the spinach and feta one) and the specialty pizzas. Breakfast fare, such as french toast, waffles, pancakes, and scrambled eggs, is also available.

Oporto Cafe, 3833 Richmond Ave., Houston, TX 77027; (713) 621-1114; www.oporto.us; Tapas; $$. If you want a side of atmosphere with your tapas and wine, head to Oporto Cafe, where Chef Richard

Di Virgilio is ready to give you a perfect European experience. When you walk in the door, expect to find more than 50 wines by the glass from Portugal, Italy, Spain, South America, and the US, as well as gourmet sandwiches, soup, salad, and tapas. Don't miss menu favorites such as steamed clams with Portuguese sausage; risotto balls served with fresh mozzarella and spicy tomato sauce; imported Spanish red peppers with herbs, crawfish, and shrimp; and baked brie with figs. Specials are offered nearly every night, including a martini and panini pairing for $10 on Monday, a 6-ounce steak and side with a glass of wine for $19 on Wednesday, and $12 paella on Sunday. There's also a wonderful happy hour.

Ouisie's Table, 3939 San Felipe St., Houston, TX 77027; (713) 528-2264; www.ouisiestable.com; Southern; $$$. Our first thought when we took our seats at this charming restaurant was how much it reminded us of the New Orleans French Quarter. It manages to be spacious and airy while also being intimate, which is a rarity in Houston. The cuisine here is considered Southern-eclectic, with menu items that include brandied oysters, a BLT wedge salad, seafood crepes, shrimp and cheese grits, panéed chicken in a crispy bread-crumb cover with Creole mustard sauce, braised short ribs au jus, and Ouisie's original chicken-fried steak with the works—a restaurant favorite. There are also daily blackboard specials, breakfast and lunch daily, and brunch on Saturday and Sunday. Brunch offerings include some of the dinner menu items as well as favorites such as cornmeal pancakes, grilled beef medallions and eggs, Ouisie's crab cake Benedict, and Ouisie's Sunset Chicken Enchiladas.

The appetizers here are wonderful as well, although I recommend against ordering them, as the restaurant offers ample complimentary bread before your meal arrives.

Pappa Bros. Steakhouse, 5839 Westheimer Rd., Houston, TX 77057; (713) 780-7352; www.pappasbros.com; Steak House; $$$$. Part of the Pappas chain of restaurants (think **Pappasitos, Pappadeaux Seafood Kitchen, Pappas Bar-B-Q,** etc.), Pappa Bros. Steakhouse is an upscale way to spend an evening. Regularly considered among the top steak houses in Houston (and that's saying a lot), Pappa Bros. serves up perfectly cooked meats in a comfortable, romantic atmosphere. Let's start with the steaks. Here you'll find a variety of cuts for around $40, including a 12-ounce filet mignon, 18-ounce rib eye, 14-ounce prime New York strip, a three-peppercorn steak, a veal chop, and a porterhouse. Sides include fresh jumbo asparagus, skillet potatoes, roasted wild mushrooms, truffle steak fries, and onion rings. And the wine list here is incredible—even if you're not drinking wine, you should check it out to see the variety. Open for dinner daily except Sunday.

Pesce, 3029 Kirby Dr., Houston, TX 77098; (713) 522-4858; www.pescehouston.com; Seafood; $$$. Sometimes it seems as if restaurateur Tilman Fertitta is involved with nearly everything in Houston. After all, he owns the Landry's group, which includes everything from the **Rainforest Cafe** to the Downtown Aquarium to Pesce. Fortunately, he has managed to give each of his restaurants its own identity, and Pesce is one of my favorites thanks to its stunning decor and incredible menu. Featuring an upscale seafood dining experience, Pesce offers gourmet fare that includes classics such as shrimp cocktail, crab cakes, and filet mignon as well as specialties infused with Southern flavor, such as gazpacho *blanco,* cornmeal-crusted redfish, oysters and jumbo shrimp, and "Big Easy" barbecued shrimp. Don't miss Chef Mark Holley's 4-course tasting menu, which includes items such as escargot *en croute,* Mediterranean salad, jerk chicken, and a chocolate brownie sundae. There is also an extensive wine list featuring more than 300 bottles.

Philippe's Restaurant, 1800 Post Oak Blvd., Ste. 200, Houston, TX 77056; (713) 439-1000; www.philippehouston.com; French; $$$. One of the newer restaurants to the Houston restaurant scene, Philippe's quickly made a name for itself thanks to its interesting menu filled with Texas adaptations of French classics. Think spicy duck confit tamales; sherried onion soup with melting gruyère; country venison pâté; salmon pizza with pickled fennel and orange vinaigrette; Texas Caesar salad with barbecue-brushed skirt steak; mussels and fries with saffron-rosemary white wine broth; baked lemon sole with savory compound butter, polenta, and truffle-port sauce; and fish and shellfish bouillabaisse with fennel, saffron, and tomato broth. With high-profile Philippe Schmit at the helm, the wonderful, casual-but-lovely restaurant is destined to become a Houston classic.

Pico's Mex-Mex, 5941 Bellaire Blvd., Houston, TX 77081; (713) 662-8383; www.picos.net; Mexican; $$. If you prefer traditional Mexican fare to the "Texanized" version you find at many restaurants here, try Pico's Mex-Mex. Since 1984, this charming hole-in-the-wall has been serving what it calls Mex-Mex food—meats cooked in banana leaves, mole, pickled red onions, *queso* made with Chihuahua cheese and topped with chorizo. There are also more traditional Tex-Mex options like enchiladas, fajitas, and tacos, as well as the requisite—and requisitely good—margaritas. Though there's lots of meat on the menu, vegetarians have options, too. The casual atmosphere makes this a good spot for families.

Pondicheri, 2800 Kirby, Ste. B132, Houston, TX 77098; (713) 522-2022; www.pondichericafe.com; Indian; $$. Even though she was already well known for seamlessly blending local Texas ingredients with classic Indian dishes at her popular restaurant, **Indika** (see p. 33), Anita Jaisinghani had another trick up her sleeve: Pondicheri. This smaller (and cheaper) little sister to Indika features a menu that was created around the street foods of India: Expect *papdi chaat* (sprouts, lentil dumplings, yogurt, and chutneys), *pakoras,* goat mince masala, and a daily selection of samosas. In terms of main dishes, the best way to order here is to get the vegetable or meat *thali,* which includes a daily selection of dishes and sides for sharing. Other items to try include

the naan with roasted garlic, the *desi* fries (french fries dusted with Indian spices), and fresh-made cookies. A counter-service breakfast and lunch are also served daily. Dinner is served from 5 to 10 p.m.

Queen Vic Pub & Kitchen, 2712 Richmond, Houston, TX 77098; (713) 533-0022; www.thequeenvicpub.com; British/Indian; $$. If you've never had the good fortune of dining on fantastic Indian food in London, there's finally a way to do it in Houston: the Queen Vic Pub & Kitchen. From its cool, sleek decor to its incredible menu, this is one of the city's greatest new places to grab some grub. Among my favorite items: short rib samosas with tamarind sweet-and-sour chutney; *saag* pizza; the Queen's Curry (Scotch egg wrapped in ground lamb in curry masala); an English burger (served with Coleman's mustard, naturally); an Indian kebab burger; wild boar sausage and mash; and fish and chips. In addition to the incredible menu, the drinks here are divine, featuring more than a dozen local and regional draft beers and a huge selection of original craft cocktails. Don't miss special events, such as beer pairings, high tea, potpie night, and Sunday roast night.

Reef, 2600 Travis, Houston, TX 77006; (713) 526-8282; www .reefhouston.com; Seafood; $$$. Chef-Owner Bryan Caswell made a huge splash (excuse the pun) in Houston when he opened this stunning restaurant, which features seafood prepared with Gulf Coast, Mediterranean, and Asian influences. Expect menu items such as steamed mussels with Shiner Bock and toasted ancho chiles, a seafood hot pot with fingerling potatoes, crispy-skin snapper with sweet and sour chard and tomato brown butter, Thai-style whole fish (limited availability), and a naked rib eye with brown butter gnocchi, arugula, and prosciutto broth. Among the sides: fried mac and cheese, corn pudding, truffled polenta with mushrooms, and toasted butter mashed potatoes. The restaurant also houses more than 1,500 bottles of wine and a variety of specialty cocktails that include kumquat mojitos and vodka-based lemonade. Closed on Sun.

Ristorante Cavour, 1080 Uptown Park Blvd. inside Hotel Granduca, Houston, TX 77056; (713) 418-1104; www.granducahouston.com; Italian; $$$. When Hotel Granduca came roaring into town a few years ago with its gold-trimmed decor and antique paintings, it was difficult to tell exactly what position this boutique hotel would hold in Houston. Thanks to Ristorante Cavour, it is earning a place on the map of Houston's best places to eat. Offering northern Italian cuisine, Ristorante Cavour is an upscale, intimate place to go for a meal—I'd recommended it as a perfect date night spot. The warm colors and small nooks and crannies give you a privacy lacking at many other Houston hot spots, and the food is so good you're going to want to share various dishes with the one you love. Consider starting with a mixed-greens salad with basil Champagne dressing, roasted pine nuts, and pear tomatoes or the pan-seared *foie gras* with roasted pear and Marsala glaze. Follow that up with homemade tagliatelle pasta with tomato coulis and extra-virgin olive oil, Maine lobster risotto, or veal osso bucco with orange sauce and Parmesan polenta. Breakfast, lunch, and brunch are also served. For Executive

Chef Renato DePirro's recipe for **Mixed Greens with Heirloom Tomatoes, Pesto Dressing, and Pine Nuts,** see p. 189, and for **Cappellacci alla Campari,** see p. 198.

Ruggles Cafe and Bakery, 2365 Rice Blvd., Houston, TX 77007; (713) 520-6662; www.rugglescafebakery.com; American; $$. Frequently overshadowed by sister restaurants such as the famous, upscale **Ruggles Grill** and the eco-friendly yet delicious **Ruggles Green** (see p. 135), Ruggles Cafe and Bakery will always hold a special place in my heart for its casual, dependable fare. Located in the popular Rice Village area, Ruggles Cafe and Bakery is a fantastic place to grab lunch during a shopping break. Expect warm baked goat cheese salad, grilled vegetable and chicken wraps, beer-battered fish tacos, and a variety of pastas and burgers. And don't forget to save room for dessert, which includes more than 2 dozen items, such as domino cakes; white chocolate bread pudding; tres leches; chocolate crème brûlée; and a variety of scones, cookies, and brownies. There's also a daily dessert special that's not offered on the regular menu. Closed Mon.

*17 Restaurant, 1117 Prairie St., Houston, TX 77002; (832) 200-8800; www.aldenhotels .comj/17.php; American; $$$. It's right in the heart of downtown, but unless you're looking for it, it can be easy to miss this great little restaurant located inside the Alden Hotel. Serving up bistro-style New American cuisine, *17 is a treat for your palate. Know what's even better? You can go nearly any time of day, from breakfast (think omelets, huevos rancheros, steak and eggs, and, my favorite, the delectable blueberry pancakes with mascarpone) to late-night dessert (don't miss the sweet potato pie with gingersnap crust and spiced ice cream). For

an initial introduction to *17, however, go for dinner, when you'll get a full taste of the chef's abilities. In addition to bistro standards such as charcuterie, upscale mac and cheese, and filet mignon, *17 also has some innovative offerings that include braised Kobe cheek with roasted cauliflower mash; olive-stuffed chicken breast with English peas, baby carrots, golden raisin and goat cheese *agnolotti,* and chicken jus; and a grilled double chop. With its rich brown interior and intimate lighting, you're likely going to want to stay awhile.

Shade, 250 W. 19th St., Houston, TX 77008; (713) 863-7500; www.shadeheights.com; Southern; $$$. For a long time this was one of the only great dining spots in the popular, up-and-coming Heights area. Great restaurants have been popping up all around in recent years, but the quality of the fare offered at this comfortable, classic, Texas-infused bistro has remained consistently good. Dinner on weekend nights can get crowded, so you may want to make reservations. Among my favorite menu items: baked eggplant and four-cheese *involtini;* risotto with seared scallops; wasabi- and cucumber-crusted red snapper; sage and garlic grilled veal chop;

and grilled beef tenderloin. The
restaurant is also open for lunch
and weekend brunch. Weekend brunch
includes a selection of fresh pastries
(think ham and cheddar hot pocket, almond bear
claw, whiskey pecan scone, etc.); homemade challah french toast;
spinach, bacon, sun-dried tomato, and cheddar quiche; and curried
tuna salad sandwich with grapes.

Sorrel Urban Bistro, 2202 W. Alabama, Houston, TX 77092;
(713) 677-0391; www.sorrelhouston.com; American; $$$. When
Sorrel Urban Bistro opened in summer 2011, Houston foodies were
excited to see exactly what restaurateur Ray Salti and Executive
Chef Soren Pedersen were up to. What they found was an organically
and locally focused menu that changes all the time depending on
what is available seasonally. There's an a la carte dinner menu (my
preference) as well as a 5-course prix fixe available. Wine pairings
are optional. There's also a 3-course prix fixe at lunch and an a la
carte Sunday brunch from 10 a.m. to 3 p.m. One of the most unique
things about this restaurant is its charcuterie bar, which offers
artisan cheeses and cut-to-order charcuterie. Sure, the charcuterie
scene has been big in Houston for several years now, but the time
and dedication paid to this charcuterie bar make it a standout. The
space is light, bright, and elegant, making it the perfect place for
anything from a date night to a family dinner. For Executive Chef
Soren Pedersen's recipe for **Grilled Rack of Lamb with Roasted
New Potato & Red Currant Demi-Glace,** see p. 196.

Spaghetti Western Italian Cafe, 1608 Shepherd Dr., Houston, TX 77007; (713) 861-4490; www.spagwesthouston.com; Italian; $$. This is the kind of place that you drive by a million times and don't stop in until one day your Italian craving gets the best of you. Once you go in, you'll be glad you did. Inspired by the spaghetti westerns of the 1960s and 1970s, this restaurant aims to offer Italian fare in a, well, Western atmosphere. Open for lunch and dinner daily, this place offers all your favorites—fried ravioli, classic calzones, pizza, pasta, and more—as well as some new favorites served with a twist. I'm a fan of the Spaghetti Western cheese steak (certified Angus beef with onions and mozzarella on a toasted hoagie); the Spaghetti Western Formal Wear (bow tie pasta tossed with chicken, sun-dried tomatoes, and mushrooms in roasted-garlic cream sauce—bonus points for the cute name); the pecan-crusted catfish topped with crawfish étouffée and served with orzo; and the Italian nachos, which are smothered in Alfredo sauce, ground sausage, mozzarella, tomatoes, black olives, green onions, and banana peppers.

Spanish Flower Mexican Restaurant, 4701 N. Main St., Houston, TX 77009; (713) 869-1706; www.spanish-flowers.com; 24-Hour Dining; $$. You never know who you're going to run into at this popular 24-hour Tex-Mex joint—everyone from local politicians to Lady Gaga has graced this lovely establishment. Why? Because the food here is top-notch. Expect Tex-Mex standards such as nachos, huevos rancheros, cheese enchiladas, and a $5.95 lunch special from 10 a.m. to 10 p.m. weekdays that includes a free bowl of soup. The atmosphere is also extremely inviting, with live music every night and a lovely outside patio that makes you feel as though you're sitting in Mexico. The restaurant also serves up traditional Mexican dishes that can be difficult to find, such as *menudo, caldo de rez,* and traditional mole. Never been? Time your visit with happy hour, between 3 and 7 p.m., when margaritas are just $2.99. Oh, and you should know that although for the most part the restaurant is open 24 hours, it does close on Tuesday at 10 p.m. and reopen Wednesday at 9 a.m.

Star Pizza, 2111 Norfolk, Houston, TX 77098; (713) 523-0800; http://starpizza.net; Italian; $$. This has long been my favorite pizza joint in Houston for one simple reason: No matter what kind of pizza you get, thin crust or deep dish, fully loaded or gluten free, the quality of the pie you receive is top-notch. Turning out pies in Houston since 1976, Star Pizza offers favorites such as Joe's (sautéed spinach and fresh garlic—try it on a whole-wheat crust), the Starburst Deluxe (pepperoni, ground beef, sausage, mushrooms, green pepper, onions, and cheese), and Ben's (ground beef, Italian sausage, pepperoni, and ham). You can also create your own pizza with toppings that include artichoke

hearts, cauliflower, goat cheese, meatballs, potatoes, salami, sun-dried tomatoes, and zucchini. Sandwiches, lasagna, pasta, salad, and desserts are also on the menu. Delivery is free. A second restaurant is located at 77 Harvard.

Revival Market's Coffee Fix

Houston's gourmet coffee scene has grown a great deal in recent years. On the roasting side, small-batch roasters such as Fusion Beans, Greenway Coffee Co., Katz's Coffee, Fontana Coffee Roasters, and Amaya Roasting Co. lead the charge for great-tasting beans in Houston. But if you're looking for a great place to go to sample those offerings, look no further than **Revival Market** (550 Heights Blvd., Houston, TX 77007; 713-880-8463; www.revivalmarket.com), which is quickly becoming the epicenter of wonderful java in the Bayou City. In addition to its excellent selection of beans, Revival Market has a huge coffee bar with menu items that include an espresso tasting flight  (plain espresso, Americano, and cappuccino) and cold-steeped iced coffee. Depending on when you go, you may even find local coffee masters moonlighting as baristas behind the counter. If you love great coffee, you don't want to miss it.

Stella Sola, 1001 Studewood St., Houston, TX 77056; (713) 880-1001; www.stellasolahouston.com; Italian; $$$. Calling its diverse selection of food "Texas Tuscan," Stella Sola is yet another excellent venture from Bryan Caswell, Houston's own celebrity chef. The menu is filled with tantalizing options that include wood-grilled Wagyu flat iron, spring lamb, sea scallops, grilled Texas quail, striped bass, and 14-ounce dry-aged strip steak, as well as such starters as roasted Gulf prawns, meat-market plate, potato gnocchi, *fritto misto,* three types of pizza, and bone marrow with condiments on house *ciabatta* toast. Dinner is served Tues through Sun. Brunch, which is less expensive but equally delicious, is served on Sun. The restaurant is closed Mon.

Strip House, 1200 McKinney, Houston, TX 77010; (713) 659-6000; www.striphouse.com/houston; Steak House; $$$. One of just a handful of Strip House restaurants in the country, Houston's version of this upscale steak house is both conveniently located and well executed. Sure, the decor is dark, but that's pretty standard for this type of restaurant. It's the food, however, that will make you want to come time and time again. Among the best items: roasted bacon salad, a very fresh Caprese salad, the potatoes Romanoff, and the filet mignon. And don't leave without trying the famous 24-layer chocolate cake, which is sure to be among the greatest chocolate cakes you've ever tasted.

Sushi Raku, 3201 Louisiana St., Houston, TX 77006; (713) 526-8885; www.sushi-raku.com; Japanese; $$$. With so many sushi options in Houston, it can be tough to narrow down a favorite. Here's where Sushi Raku stands out. In addition to offering a stunning, inviting ambience, the food is fresh—as in flown-in-from-Tokyo fresh. Between owner Patrick Chiu, who has more than 13 years of experience in the Japanese restaurant industry, and

Chef Taka Sekiguchi, who has worked with some of the best chefs in Japan, you can be sure you're going to have a very memorable experience. Expect all of your favorite sushi dishes as well as some surprises, such as rib eye, pork jowl and bacon-wrapped scallop skewers, and duck soba-noodle soup. Looking for a great deal? Go during happy hour, when a variety of rolls and skewers start at around $4. Don't miss the fantastic Cajun roll, the Kobe slider, or the simple but delicious edamame. The cocktails, such as the lychee martini, are also fantastic.

Tacos a Go Go, 3704 Main St., Houston, TX 77002; (713) 807-8226; www.tacosagogo.com; Tex-Mex; $. Don't let the whimsical murals and kitschy decor fool you: This place takes its food seriously. Come here for fresh flour, corn, and whole-wheat tortillas stuffed with ingredients such as grilled Alaskan pollock, shredded chicken breast, mixed veggies with black beans, tender shredded lamb, and beef stew in tomato sauce. The menu also includes Tex-Mex favorites such as breakfast tacos, *migas,* huevos rancheros, quesadillas, burritos, and combination plates of items such as soft tacos, tamales, tostadas, nachos, and gorditos. Mexican sodas, mimosas, sangria, and beer are also offered. Need a late-night fix after an evening out on the town? This is the place for you. On Fri and Sat, Tacos a Go Go is open until 2 a.m.

T'Afia, 3701 Travis St., Houston, TX 77002; (713) 524-6922; www.tafia.com; American; $$$. This is the headquarters of Chef Monica Pope, one of Houston's most celebrated chefs, known for her stylish, local-focused brand of cooking. Take a seat at the lovely outside patio and get ready to eat, because the menu here is perfect for ordering multiple dishes and sharing with friends. Among my favorites on the menu: mix-and-match appetizers that include olives, split-pea hummus, beet and orange ceviche, and a variety of cheeses; and small plates such as mushroom dumplings, Real Ale brown ale–battered creminis, and tuna and salmon sashimi. My favorite entrees include shrimp and tuna fricassee; balsamic caramel beef cubes with peppers and onions; and portobello piccata with greens, caper blossoms, and lemon sauce. In addition to dinner, the restaurant also offers a Friday lunch and occasional brunch.

III Forks, 1201 San Jacinto St., Houston, TX 77002; (713) 658-9457; www.iiiforks.com; Steak House; $$$. One of just a half dozen III Forks locations in the country, this downtown hot spot features a classic steak house vibe in a very hip atmosphere. In the bustling Houston Pavilions area of downtown, you can expect an upbeat, fun crowd and really tasty food when you come here. Prices are pretty comparable to most steak houses in town—expect to pay at least $35 or $40 per person—but the steak alone makes it worth the trip. Options include filet mignon, bone-in rib eye, and New York strip. Not into steak? Never fear: The roasted chicken with red pepper sauce, double-cut pork chop, prime burger with fries, and vegetable ravioli are also standouts. And don't miss the melt-in-your-mouth dessert options, which include bread pudding, Texas pecan cake, and crème brûlée. Other must-try items on the menu include the six-cheese potatoes; the III Forks salad; and the seafood medley appetizer, which comes with shrimp cocktail, crab cake St. Francis, and bacon-wrapped scallop. In terms of wine, there are 1,500 bottles from around the world in the sprawling wine cellar, which is kept at 58 degrees. White wines are stored at 45 degrees in an additional on-site cooler.

Tila's Restaurant and Bar, 1111 S. Shepherd Dr., Houston, TX 77019; (713) 522-7654; www.tilas.com; Mexican; $$$. One of Houston's top-tier Mexican restaurants, Tila's features everything you could hope for in a south of the border–dedicated hot spot. "If Cheech Marin and Frida Kahlo ever had a daughter, she'd probably grow up to open a place like Tila's," the website says. My dinners here typically start with margaritas (fresh-squeezed lime juice, Grand Marnier, and salt, naturally) and end, inexplicably, with wine. It's the kind of place where you'll want to linger over a starter of *queso fundido* (their version comes with melted white cheese, roasted poblano chile, tomatoes, fresh onions, and mushrooms), followed by some delightful *chilaquiles,* blackened halibut, or *carne asada.* At this Houston institution since the 1980s, with more

than 60 types of premium tequilas, a visit here almost always promises a great time. If the weather is nice, grab a spot on the lush porch. Brunch and happy hour specials are also available. Oh, and don't miss the drool-inducing desserts, which include coconut flan, Mexican lime pie, crepes with *cajeta* Mexican caramel, and *tres chocolates:* three layers of dark, semisweet fudge crisps, white chocolate, and mousse with almond slivers and chocolate savings.

Tiny Boxwood's, 3614 W. Alabama St., Houston, TX 77027; (713) 622-4224; www.thompsonhanson.com; Breakfast; $$. Okay, so the actual cafe space is tiny and parking can be a total pain, but once you sit down at a table, chances are good that you'll be completely charmed by this hidden gem in the heart of River Oaks. This place is ideal for lunch—if the weather's nice, grab a seat outside. Menu items here include a summer salad of mixed greens, grilled chicken, apples, blue cheese crumbles, candied pecans, and apple cider vinaigrette; the Frenchman sandwich with thinly sliced prosciutto layered between diced tomatoes, goat cheese, and basil pesto on hot sourdough; and the Just Beet It Burger, a slow-roasted beet and black bean patty with chipotle aioli on a toasted white bun. Breakfast, brunch, and dinner are also served. Whatever you do, don't leave without grabbing a delicious homemade chocolate chip cookie—they are amazing.

Treebeards, 315 Travis St., Houston, TX 77002; (713) 228-2622; www.treebeards.com; Southern; $$. The name of the game here is true, authentic Southern cuisine, and, man, it is good. The Market Square location, which is probably the restaurant's most popular, is located in a building that has been standing since 1861 and is the second-oldest building in Houston. That historical fact makes it worth a visit in and of itself, but more than that, the reason to come to Treebeards is the wonderful food. Expect incredible red beans and rice (a vegetarian variety is also served); jambalaya; shrimp with étouffée; and daily specials that include jerk chicken, a stuffed pork chop, chicken-fried chicken with gravy, and blackened catfish. My favorite dish here? The duck gumbo with a side of corn bread, followed by an incredible slice of gooey butter cake. You can't beat it. Additional locations are at 1117 Texas and 1100 Louisiana in the downtown tunnel.

Truluck's Restaurant, 5350 Westheimer Rd., Houston, TX 77056; (713) 783-7270; www.trulucks.com; Steak House; $$$. When it comes to steak houses in Houston, there are so many great ones that you start to wonder if the larger, national chains can compete. The answer to this question, at least when it comes to Truluck's, is yes. When you walk in the door at this upscale eatery, you feel instantly at ease thanks to the classy yet comfortable atmosphere. But it's after you sit down that the real fun begins. One item that you can't miss a chance to order is the Maine Jonah crab claw platter, which comes with 8 delicious claws. Other menu standouts include the salt and pepper calamari; the Sonoma greens salad (spicy Texas pecans with goat cheese, tart apples, kalamata olives, and honey vinaigrette); the sautéed falafel (perfect for vegetarians); and the blackened redfish Pontchartrain with crawfish tails, Gulf shrimp, and blue crab in a spicy Creole sauce. The power lunch, which is $25 and comes with a soup or a salad, an entree, and dessert, is another great way to try out the restaurant.

Valentino Vin Bar Houston, 2525 W. Loop South, Houston, TX 77027; (866) 292-4100; www.hotelderek.com/valentino; Italian; $$$. With its modern decor, drenched in reds and grays, Valentino Vin Bar Houston is inviting from the minute you walk in the door. And regardless of whether you're staying in the adjacent Hotel Derek or dropping by for a quick bite during happy hour, you won't be disappointed with the fare served up here. The restaurant is operated by Owner–Executive Chef Luciano Pellegrini and owner Piero Selvaggio, two pillars of the Italian-American restaurant scene. When you come here, you can expect incredible, authentic Italian cuisine and an extensive wine list. Among the menu highlights: sliced prosciutto with cantaloupe salad; Texas smoked quail arugula salad; a *pesce crudo* with ahi tuna with *cren* aioli, passion fruit white tuna, pompano lemon sauce, and green apple scallops; seared Scottish salmon, oven potatoes, and puttanesca sauce; a veal chop with asparagus, prosciutto, Asiago, and demi sauce; and a selection of delicious pastas such as egg fettuccine with meat sauce, penne pasta with pancetta, Parmesan, egg yolk, and cream, and spaghetti with shrimp, tomato, and basil. Breakfast, lunch, and a cocktails and tapas menu are also available. For Valentino Vin Bar's recipe for **Lobster Mezzeluna,** see p. 194.

Vic & Anthony's, 1510 Texas Ave., Houston, TX 77002; (713) 228-1111; www.vicandanthonys.com; Steak House; $$$$. A favorite among Houston Astros players because of its proximity to Minute Maid Park (this is one of former Astro Hunter Pence's top places to hang out), Vic & Anthony's is another of the best-rated steak houses in Houston. Why? For starters, owner Tilman Fertitta traveled across the country with his father looking for the country's best steak houses and put the best of what he found into practice at Vic & Anthony's. Standout items here include the steaks (obviously), particularly the filet mignon and the prime rib eye. In terms of appetizers, you can't go wrong with the steak tartare with chips, cornichons, and whole-grain mustard; the fresh oysters; or the artisan cured-meat sampler. The seafood here is also a highlight: Consider the Gulf red snapper with jumbo lump crab and baby vegetables, the cold-water lobster tail, or the Szechuan pepper-crusted tuna with soy ginger butter sauce (my favorite). Sides include fantastic au gratin potatoes, buttered broccoli, and onion strings. Open daily for dinner; reservations are recommended.

Voice Restaurant and Lounge, Hotel ICON, 220 Main St., Houston, TX 77002; (713) 224-4266; www.hotelicon.com; American; $$$$. Voice epitomizes fine dining. The beautifully decorated restaurant is located downtown inside Hotel ICON, and it's not just the restaurant and lounge's appearance (or the cowhide-backed barstools) that count here; Chef Michael Kramer also places considerable emphasis on the presentation of the food, which includes plenty of seafood, lamb, duck, chicken, and beef options. Everything is made and embellished with produce from local farmers' markets, but vegetarians don't have many options, aside from salad and appetizers. Those who dine in the lounge have their pick of cheeses, crab cakes, and fish and chips made with tuna tartare. The restaurant also serves breakfast.

Willie G's Steakhouse and Seafood, 1605 Post Oak Blvd., Houston, TX 77056; (713) 840-7190; www.williegs.com; Seafood; $$$. They serve a variety of dishes here, but the reason I come is, understandably, for the seafood. This upscale steak and seafood joint has a gorgeous, recently remodeled patio and an innovative menu that makes it feel both classic and food-forward. The dinner menu alone reads like a seafood dictionary: iced seafood tower of chilled lobster, jumbo cocktail shrimp, fresh oysters, and king crab; seafood-stuffed jalapeños; seafood filé gumbo; grilled salmon *cerreto,* topped with roasted mushrooms and drizzled with lemon butter; and a selection of fresh fish including red snapper, flounder, mahimahi, Chilean sea bass, swordfish, and golden tile. There's also a happy hour menu offered from 3 to 7 p.m. that includes $1.95 hot bites such as onion strings and fried zucchini; $3.95 raw-bar specialties include a half-dozen Gulf oysters and a half-dozen peel-and-eat shrimp; $4.95 munchies such as Willie's chili minidogs with homemade chili, cheddar, and onion, and sushi shrimp skewers with citrus chili sauce; and $5.95 pulled pork, buffalo chicken, and all-beef sliders.

Zelko Bistro, 705 E. 11th St., Houston, TX 77008; (713) 880-8691; www.zelkobistro.com; Southern; $$. The first thing that strikes you about this restaurant, which was built into a 1920s bungalow, is that it's like walking into a mix of an antiques shop and your grandma's kitchen. The structure itself has been largely preserved but updated (Ball jar lights, refinished sinks), and the outside has been landscaped with fresh herbs, cedar fences, and a garden. But it's the food here that will really get to you. The brain-child of Chef-Owner Jamie Zelko, this casual little bistro serves up a mix of comfort classics such as grilled tuna salad, fried pickles, fried chicken, meat loaf, and Saint Arnold's beer–soaked short ribs. Brunch fare includes a chicken and waffle, Gas House eggs (farm eggs in brioche, potatoes, and bacon or sausage), an egg sandwich, and the Bungalow breakfast (2 eggs with toast, potatoes, and applewood-smoked bacon or sausage). Brunch is served on weekends. The restaurant is closed Mon.

The Breakfast Klub, 3711 Travis St., Houston, TX 77002; (713) 528-8561; www.breakfastklub.com; Breakfast; $$. If you've got a hankering for breakfast, you absolutely can't miss the opportunity to dine at The Breakfast Klub, which for years has been Houston's most famous morning eatery. In addition to traditional fare such as biscuits and gravy, french toast, and omelets, the restaurant also offers unique combinations such as Katfish and Grits (catfish fillet with grits, potatoes, or eggs, and choice of toast or biscuit), Wings and Waffle (6 chicken wing pieces and a Belgian waffle topped with fresh strawberries and powdered sugar), and Green Eggs and Ham (2 eggs with chives, spinach, and bell peppers with potatoes or grits and toast or biscuit). Granted, you'll probably have to wait in line, particularly if you come here on a weekend morning, but trust me—it's worth the wait.

Brennan's, 3300 Smith St., Houston, TX 77006; (713) 522-9711; www.brennanshouston.com; Southern; $$$. To truly appreciate a visit to Brennan's, it's important to know the backstory of this Houston institution, which opened in 1967 as a sister restaurant to the famous Commander's Palace in New Orleans. It offered up the city's best Texas Creole offerings for decades until September 2008, when a fire caused indirectly by Hurricane Ike destroyed the building. Now Brennan's has reopened in the same location and is offering the same reliable, delicious favorites it always has. Start with the incredible Breaux Bridge crawfish and corn soup and a barbecued Louisiana crawfish shortcake, followed by porcini-crusted veal and crawfish with a side of roasted asparagus. For dessert order the famous bananas Foster. The restaurant is also open for lunch Mon through Fri and for brunch on weekends.

Hugo's, 1600 Westheimer Rd., Houston, TX 77006; (713) 524-7744; www.hugosrestaurant.net; Tex-Mex; $$$. From the first time I walked into Hugo's, I was in love. The decor is traditional yet contemporary, the staff is welcoming, and the regional Mexican cuisine served here is the best of the best. Headed by Executive Chef Hugo Ortega, Hugo's offers a wonderful variety of south of the border favorites that can be difficult to find elsewhere. Expect fresh seafood appetizers such as a crabmeat cocktail with cucumber, watermelon, and avocado, inspired soups and salads, and entrees such as grilled snapper tacos, achiote-rubbed tender suckling pig, and roasted goat. If you can make it here for only one meal, however, make it brunch, when the best of Hugo's offerings are all out on display. A select brunch menu is offered on Saturday; a brunch buffet is available on Sunday.

Kenny and Ziggy's Deli, 2327 Post Oak Blvd., Houston, TX 77056; (713) 871-8883; www.kennyandziggys.com; American; $$. If you ever find yourself craving pastrami, matzo balls, and blintzes, this is the place for you. This New York–style deli has been a local institution since it opened its doors in 1999. The menu features more than 200 items ranging from traditional deli items (corned beef, bagel and lox platters, tuna melt, steak burger) to surprising fare (Genghis Cohen's Chinese Chicken Salad, Fan Tan Fannie's Famous Snapper, English-style fish and chips). Guy Fieri, host of the Food Network's

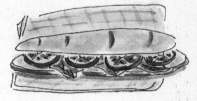

Diners, Drive-Ins, and Dives, was so impressed that he featured the restaurant in a recent show. There's also a full range of breakfast items, including omelets, potato pancakes, steak and eggs, and daily specials.

Mai's, 3403 Milam St., Houston, TX 77002; (713) 520-5300; www.maishouston.com; Vietnamese; $. Founded in 1978, Mai's Restaurant has long been a Houston institution known for serving some of the best Vietnamese and Chinese food in the country. When a fire destroyed the restaurant in February 2010, the Nguyen family vowed to rebuild. And rebuild they did, opening a glossier, more updated, but just as authentic restaurant last April. Expect to find an interesting, varied menu that includes spring rolls, fried chicken wings, curry chicken wing stew, Vietnamese noodle soup, fried rice, stir-fried noodles, a variety of tofu dishes, and even Vietnamese fajitas served with fresh lettuce, cucumber, carrots, bean sprouts, mint, cilantro, and rice paper. The restaurant is closed Sun.

Niko Niko's, 2520 Montrose, Houston, TX 77006; (713) 528-4976; www.nikonikos.com; Greek; $$. I had been hearing about this place since the day I first moved to Houston, so when I finally visited for lunch on a busy Saturday, I figured there was no way it could possibly live up to the hype. I was wrong. So wrong. This Greek-American cafe offers spot-on interpretations of the greatest Greek dishes, including perfectly seasoned gyros, lamb kebabs, dolmades, spanakopita, and combination platters. Don't forget to start with an order of hummus with pita or feta fries. Oh, and if you can try only one thing on the menu, make it the chicken avgolemono soup, which is filled with tender chicken, rice, and vegetables in a light lemon broth. The menu prices can be a little high, but the servings are enormous—if you go for lunch, you'll have more than enough left over for dinner. A second location is at 301 Milam.

The Original Ninfa's on Navigation, 2704 Navigation Blvd., Houston, TX 77003; (713) 977-4000; www.mamaninfas.com; Tex-Mex; $$. In the scope of Tex-Mex restaurants, Ninfa's has become an important piece of the Houston scene, with locations peppering the city and the state. But for an authentic Houston experience, there's nothing like a visit to the Original Ninfa's on Navigation, where the food is always first-rate and even the servers here are viewed as local celebrities. Operated by Chef Alex Padilla, the restaurant serves up dependable, delicious fare. Expect fresh homemade tortillas, handmade tamales, and menu offerings that range from crispy calamari tossed with ancho and serrano chiles to shredded-chicken soup to taco platters that will leave you full for days. Don't miss the tacos *al carbon*—they are legendary. And thanks to a recent renovation of the outside patio, it's a better place than ever to linger with a margarita.

Rainbow Lodge, 2011 Ella Blvd., Houston, TX 77008; (713) 861-8666; www.rainbow-lodge.com; Southern; $$$. The name of the game here is, well, game. Namely wild game, which takes on many incarnations on the menu, such as tomato-simmered wild boar meatballs over creamy Parmesan polenta; American bison brisket pot roast; butter-roasted Nilgai antelope; and mixed grill of venison medallion, 15-hour smoked lamb shoulder, Texas quail, and wild boar chop. Not into game? No worries. There's also a wide selection of seafood (don't miss the crispy, crunchy rainbow trout), fowl, and other meats. One of my favorite things about Rainbow Lodge (in addition to its fabulous patio) is that it holds fun, innovative special events, such as its occasional patio wine tastings and casual Sunday suppers, which feature comfort food and half-price wines by the glass.

RDG Bar Annie, 1800 Post Oak Blvd., Houston, TX 77056; (713) 840-1111; www.rdgbarannie.com; American; $$$. Long one of Houston's most famous restaurants, owned by super Chef Robert Del Grande, RDG Bar Annie recently underwent a huge renovation that transitioned it from the longtime legend Cafe Annie to RDG. The fare remains consistent and cutting edge, but the decor is now bright, airy, and very inviting. There are so many reasons to come to RDG—the Sunday brunch, the Sunday dinner (think an upscale community dinner like your grandmother would make, if your grandmother were Audrey Hepburn), and the affordable lunch. But I recommended starting at dinner, when all the best that RDG has to offer is on display. Start with a lemon melon martini or a Sangarita (that's sangria mixed with a margarita) at Bar Annie, then head to your table, where appetizers such as black bean dip with Spanish chorizo, jalapeños and goat cheese, bacon-wrapped Texas quail with jalapeño and buttermilk dressing, and Asian nachos with yellowtail sashimi with avocado and ginger await. For a main course, consider the wood-grilled redfish with Texas oyster–corn bread dressing; the wood-roasted rabbit enchiladas and red mole sauce; or wood-grilled Colorado lamb chops with fresh thyme, black pepper tomato jelly, and giant corona beans.

Tony's, 3755 Richmond Ave., Houston, TX 77046; (713) 622-6778; www.tonyshouston.com; Italian; $$$$. A foodie's visit to Tony's, probably the most famous and most upscale restaurant in Houston, is as important as an art lover's visit to the Louvre—it's something everyone must do once. Yes, it'll be expensive. Yes, you need to dress up. And yes, you should make a reservation. But even if you're most comfortable in casual cafes, you won't soon forget your meal at this world-class Italian-American eatery. From the beautiful decor (filled with important contemporary art) to a wine list with more than 1,100 options, the details here count. And the menu is to die for. Think a variety of 40-day naturally aged steaks; seafood ranging from Gulf Coast flounder to whole roasted *branzino;* and appetizers including a wild salmon tower, lobster bisque, and warm spinach salad carbonara. There's also a lunch menu, a late-night menu, and a chef's tasting menu with 3 courses for $65 a person. The restaurant is open daily.

Specialty Stores, Markets & Producers

The Acadian Bakery, 604 W. Alabama, Houston, TX 77006; (713) 520-1484; www.acadianbakers.com. The Acadian Bakery calls itself Houston's "baker to the stars," and given the lineup of people who have enjoyed a slice of cake or a tender pastry from this shop, that's probably a fair slogan: Everyone from George H. W. Bush and Arnold Schwarzenegger to Elizabeth Taylor and Reba McEntire has nibbled on goods from this bakery. Owned by Sandra Bubbert, the Acadian Bakery offers a wide variety of wonderful cakes, including a Louisiana praline (light vanilla cake with Louisiana praline liquor and French buttercream icing with New Orleans praline pieces), the signature brownie chocolate mousse (rich brownie cake with light chocolate mousse filling, chocolate or white buttercream icing, or chocolate ganache), English lemon curd (light vanilla cake with lemon curd topping and filling, with buttercream icing), and fresh strawberry (light vanilla cake with layers of strawberries and cream, French buttercream icing, white chocolate shavings, and chocolate-dipped strawberries). Special-occasion cakes are also available for nearly any holiday. An on-site deli offers lunch fare and wonderful box lunches.

Catalina Coffee, 2201 Washington Ave., Houston, TX 77007; (713) 861-8448; www.catalinacoffeeshop.com. Since it opened in April 2007, Catalina Coffee has been serving some of the best coffee brews and blends in town. But what makes this place really special is its dedication to expert roasting. Most of the coffee featured here is from Amaya Roasting Company, although Catalina also frequently  brings in guest coffees from around the country. The shop also sells a variety of brewing items including French presses, coffee drippers, and vacuum pots. Hungry? Try one of their cookies, muffins, or croissants. This neighborhood coffee shop can't be beat for your early morning cup of joe.

Central Market Houston, 3815 Westheimer Rd., Houston, TX 77027; (713) 386-1700; www.centralmarket.com. Looking for a hard-to-find olive oil? A unique wine? The absolute freshest seafood? No matter what you're seeking, from inspiration for Sunday dinner to a fun gift for your favorite foodie, it's a good bet that Central Market will have it. It's like a food lover's dream grocery store come to life. Every time I walk in, I am overwhelmed by the number of products on the shelves that I never even knew existed. In addition to being the go-to place for hard-to-find products, Central Market is also a great place to go for inspiration. From a regular Hatch chile celebration to cooking classes that will have you whipping up dishes like a professional, you'll become a better cook—and foodie—each time you visit. Added bonus: Central Market focuses on fresh, organic produce and prides itself on incorporating local companies into everything it does.

The Chocolate Bar, 1835 W. Alabama St., Houston, TX 77098; (713) 520-8599; www.theoriginalchocolatebar.com. The overpowering smell of deliciousness hits you the minute you walk through the door of this wonderful candy-loving institution that looks like it could have been created by Willy Wonka himself. Featuring everything from made-to-order specialty chocolate pizzas to incredible cakes (do not miss Aunt Etta's fudge cake) and cookies to ice cream in flavors such as Nutter Butter, root beer float, and German chocolate, the Chocolate Bar is the place to go for any of your chocolate needs. Looking for a gift idea? The shop also has a variety of innovative chocolate figures for everyone from the dog lover to the lawyer in your life. A second location is at 2521 University Blvd.

City Hall Farmers' Market, 901 Bagby St., Houston, TX 77002; www.urbanharvest.org. Like to mix work and pleasure? If you work downtown, pop over to this new-on-the-scene market, which is held every Wednesday from 10 a.m. to 2 p.m. and features more than 40 vendors. In addition to grabbing local produce, meats, and cheeses, you can also find prepared lunch items, such as Indian plate lunches, crepes, fusion tacos, vegan tamales, hamburgers, quiche, and more. It's a really fun way to break up your workday and meet other community-minded individuals.

Crave Cupcakes, 5600 Kirby Dr., Houston, TX 77005; (713) 622-7283; www.cravecupcakes.com. The boutique cupcake shop trend is still going strong in Houston, and out of the chains that have made their way to our city, Crave Cupcakes is my favorite, featuring a line of perfectly moist, perfectly iced cupcakes in flavors such as candy bar, chocolate on vanilla, coconut, cranberry orange, gluten-free chocolate, Nutella, peanut butter chocolate, red velvet, strawberry, and vanilla on chocolate. I'm also a big fan of the breakfast flavors here, which include apple streusel, gingerbread, lemon poppy seed, and maple walnut. If you have kids, be sure to take them so they can watch as the bakers systematically press out adorable fondant cupcake toppers. Mini-cupcakes are also available by preorder. A second location is at 1151 Uptown Park Blvd.

Dacapo's Pastry Cafe, 1141 E. 11th St., Houston, TX 77009; (713) 869-9141; www.dacapospastrycafe.com. When you drive past Dacapo's Pastry Cafe in the Heights, you're likely to see people sitting outside enjoying delicious soups and sandwiches that alone offer a good reason to come here. But if you're seeking the true Dacapo's experience, you have to go for the pastries, which include cakes (Italian cream, German chocolate, strawberry cream, red velvet, fresh pear, and sour cream coffee cake, to name a few), pies (pecan, cinnamon pecan, Dutch apple, key lime, etc.), cookies, brownies, cupcakes, cinnamon rolls, sweet breads, croissants, and more. Don't miss the incredible carrot cake, pumpkin maple cream cake, or the banana split cake. They also do wedding cakes that come highly recommended. Open daily except Sun.

Houston Dairymaids, 2201 Airline Dr., Houston, TX 77009; (713) 880-4800; www.houstondairymaids.com. The Houston Dairymaids are just one example of what makes this city so special. Dedicated to finding and exposing artisan cheesemakers in the local area, this small, hardworking business has ingrained itself in Houston, forcing stores and restaurateurs to reconsider the products they carry. Most of the cheeses spotlighted by the Dairymaids are made naturally by hand and created with unpasteurized milk. Cheese tastings are held at the Dairymaid warehouse, 2201 Airline Dr., on Friday and Saturday. You can also find the Dairymaids at the Houston Farmers' Market at Rice University on Tues from 3:30 to 7 p.m.; the Midtown Farmers' Market at T'Afia on Sat from 8 a.m. to noon; and at Grogan's Mill Village in The Woodlands on Sat from 8 a.m. to noon in the fall. You can also order many of the products directly from the Dairymaids website.

Houston Farmers' Market, 3016 White Oak Blvd. at Onion Creek Coffee House, Houston, TX 77007; www.localharvest.com. Open every Saturday from 8 a.m. to noon, this small but powerful farmers' market is filled with items such as homemade baked goods, fresh flowers, handmade crafts, and more. Once you're finished shopping, head inside to **Onion Creek Coffee House,** which offers a full gourmet coffee bar and breakfast items such as scones, croissants, waffles, breakfast tacos, breakfast paninis, and bagel sandwiches. Coming later in the day? There's a full lunch and dinner menu as well as beer and wine. Happy hour is daily from 4 to 7 p.m.

Katz Coffee, 1003 W. 34th St., Houston, TX 77018; (713) 864-3338; www.katzcoffee.com. This small batch fair-traded coffee roaster was founded in Houston in 2003, creating blends for some of the area's most popular restaurants. It now serves local institutions such as

Agora Cafe, Benjy's (see p. 5), **Empire Cafe** (see p. 23), **Inversion Cafe, Kraftsmen Baking** (see below), **Niko Niko's** (see p. 71), and **The Tasting Room** (see p. 96). The business has also expanded to provide roasts all across Texas in cities such as Austin, San Antonio, Galveston, and McAllen. You can also buy Katz Coffee at the **Midtown Farmers' Market** (see p. 82), **Central Market** (see p. 76), and **Whole Foods Market** (see p. 89).

Kraftsmen Baking, 4100C Montrose, Houston, TX 77006; (713) 524-3737; www.kraftsmenbaking.com. Made from high-quality and frequently organic ingredients, the delicious baked goods coming out of Kraftsmen Baking are at once tender, crunchy, and perfectly seasoned. Both a retail and wholesale operation, Kraftsmen Baking is a good place to grab one of 13 signature sandwiches for lunch, place a wholesale order, or get your event catered; box lunches are also available. You can also find Kraftsmen products at the **Midtown Farmers' Market** (see p. 82). Favorite menu items here include pastries, sandwiches, fresh-baked bread, of course, cookies, tacos, and cinnamon rolls.

Marble Slab Creamery, 3175 W. Holcombe, Houston, TX 77025; (713) 668-0431; www.marbleslab.com. This ice cream shop now has locations all over the world, but it all started in Houston in 1983 with a chef-driven vision to offer premium ice cream to the masses. The result is a smooth, creamy product that leaves you craving scoop after scoop after scoop. Signature flavors here include chocolate swiss, strawberry, vanilla cinnamon, peanut butter banana, butter pecan, fudge (that's rich fudge sauce mixed with sweet-cream ice cream), rum, mango, bubblegum, black walnut, key lime, pistachio, and black cherry. Need to top it off? Consider everything from chocolate-covered raisins to Whoppers to Ding Dongs to shredded coconut. My favorite is the Snickerdoodle: vanilla with Snickers and caramel. There's also a wide selection of cakes including the cookie dough drizzle, a smooth mint masterpiece, sweet cream and strawberries, tiramisu crunch cake, and swiss cocoa buttercup. We've made a tradition of getting our holiday cakes here, and we have never been disappointed. Want to try it out? There are more than four dozen Marble Slab Creamery locations in the Houston area. If you plan to visit often, be sure to grab a frequent buyer card, which qualifies you for freebies and special promotions. Check website for additional locations.

Midtown Farmers' Market, 3701 Travis St. at T'Afia, Houston, TX 77002; www.tafia.com. Self-dubbed a "foodie paradise and morning party," the weekly Midtown Farmers' Market is a great place to pick up a few things or find inspiration for your next dinner party. In addition to offering hot breakfast, fresh-baked breads, cheeses, mimosas, and on-site knife sharpening (don't mix those last two), the market is also a favorite among Houston's elite chef community. That guy standing next to you? He very well could be opening the next big restaurant in Houston. Held in the parking lot outside Chef Monica Pope's famous restaurant, **T'Afia** (see p. 60), it just makes sense that her foodie friends and fans would congregate. It's held every Sat from 8 a.m. to noon.

Moeller's Bakery, 4201 Bellaire Blvd., Houston, TX 77025; (713) 667-0983; www.moellersbakery.com. Open since 1930, this is another Houston institution that gets it right with to-die-for cakes and baked goods. The petits fours here will stick in your memory for years—they're light and airy, and melt in your mouth. The orange rolls, gingerbread men, cookies, and fruit Danishes are also incredible. Need to order a special-occasion cake? Don't miss the plain white cake, which is perfectly baked deliciousness.

Nundini Italian Market and Deli, 500 N. Shepherd Dr., Houston, TX 77007; (713) 861-6331; www.nundini.com. This little market-meets-cafe is a gold mine if you're looking for anything in the Italian food genre. Stroll through the wide market area, where imported goods including pasta, sauces, syrups, meats, cheeses, coffees, teas, wines, and pastries are ready to greet you. Want something on the spot? Turn to the deli and cafe, where options include smoked salmon, grilled veggie, and roast beef panini; Greek, tuna, and Caprese salads; pasta salads; and gelato in flavors such as almond with marzipan cherries, *dolce de leche*, cardamom, lemon, hazelnut, and tiramisu. Occasional wine tastings are also offered.

One Green Street, 5160 Buffalo Speedway, Houston, TX 77005; (281) 888-9518; www.onegreenstreet.com. This new little store is dedicated to being an "organic lifestyle destination," meaning that you can come here for all of your needs, from body care products and bedding to jewelry and accessories. In addition, there's plenty for the food lover, from organic, fair-traded coffee to fantastic snacks such as Lemon Blue Agave Grawnola by Hail Merry; organic, fair-traded 45 percent milk chocolate by Theo Chocolates; Cinnamon Chocolate Mexicano by Taza Chocolates; and even a chocolate and beer pairing kit. Owner Sherry Eichberger is dedicated to trying to transform people's lives, both inside and out, with her products. It's definitely worth a stop in. The store is open daily except Mon.

Picnic, 1928 Bissonnet St., Houston, TX 77005; (713) 524-0201; www.picnicboxlunches.com. Not only is this place adorable, with its bright striped awning and fun interior, but it's also a very smart concept: Picnic is a neighborhood cafe and bakery that also makes box lunches for the masses. And these aren't just any

box lunches. They're gourmet box lunches, with homemade breads, cookies, salads, and sandwiches. For $8.50, you get your choice of sandwich that can include roast beef, egg salad, char-grilled veggie, and pork tenderloin, to name a few, with fruit salad, chips, a cookie, and a pickle. Other offerings include a soup of the day (varies daily but could include chicken vegetable, lentil, or black bean) and box salads (including Greek chicken salad, spinach salad, and chef salad). Whether you order ahead for a company lunch or drop in solo for a bite, you'll enjoy time spent at Picnic. Open daily except Sun.

Pie in the Sky Pie Co., 632 W. 19th St., Houston, TX 77009; (713) 864-3301; www.pieintheskypieco.com. First things first: We need to talk about the pie. Particularly the sour cream raisin pie, which I tried at the urging of a friend even though it sounded disgusting to me. The truth? It was fantastic, like a light, airy, flavorful cheesecake. My favorite thing to do when I visit Pie in the Sky Pie Co. with friends is to order a pie sampler platter that allows you to try 4 types of pie on one plate. With varieties such as vanishing blueberry, chocolate peanut butter, lemon cream, no sugar added apple, and strawberry rhubarb, you really can't go wrong. Not that into pie? A full selection of sandwiches, wraps, burgers, soups, salads, and other items is also available. Don't miss the incredible lime cilantro chicken sandwich (char-grilled chicken breast with creamy cilantro dressing, swiss cheese, lettuce, and tomato on an herb bun) or the delicious strawberry spinach salad (with sweet olive oil and sesame seed dressing and topped with fresh berries and grilled chicken breast in jerk sauce). A second location is at 3600 N. Loop 336 West in Conroe.

Raia's Italian Market, 4500 Washington Ave., Ste. 200, Houston, TX 77007; (713) 861-1042; www.raiasitalianmarket.com. Despite the name, this place is mostly a restaurant, with a diverse menu that includes classic Italian fare such as sausage and peppers, fresh fried mozzarella, chicken Parmesan, lasagna, puttanesca, blue crab ravioli, and a variety of pizzas and sandwiches. But if you're cooking up an Italian meal at home and want to grab a few things, this is also a good place to turn, thanks to a small but well-stocked deli and market area. Products include bread sticks, olive oil, meatballs, and gelato. Also, it's worth mentioning that this place is BYOB.

Revival Market, 550 Heights Blvd., Houston, TX 77007; (713) 880-8463; www.revivalmarket.com. Yet another testament to Houston's thriving food scene, Revival Market opened in the Heights in early 2011 with much fanfare. It specializes in Texas-produced products such as meats, produce, eggs, house-made sauces, cheeses, breads, etc. There's also a small cafe serving breads, pastries, sandwiches, and breakfast tacos. The BLT—made with seasoned mayonnaise and crispy bacon—is a highlight. Walking into Revival Market is like venturing into a wonderful farmers' market that's open every day. Think of it as a wonderful, local alternative to **Central Market** (see p. 76) and **Whole Foods** (see p. 89). Don't miss the chance to have a bite on the outdoor patio.

Rice University Farmers' Market, 2100 University Blvd. on Rice University campus, Houston, TX 77005; http://farmersmarket .rice.edu. Dedicated to providing an outlet for local farmers and giving the public a place to grab wonderful organic and locally grown food, the Rice University Farmers' Market has become one of the best places to stroll in the city. Open every Tues from 3:30 to 7 p.m., the market features products such as gluten-free baked goods, coffee, cheese, soaps, free-range eggs, fish, pure, local honey, hand-cured bacon, goat milk, lavender-based products, fresh-baked dog and cat treats, organic baby food, soup, and even gelato.

Slow Dough Bread Co., (713) 568-5674; www.slowdough breadco.com. You can't really visit Slow Dough Bread Co., but they're worth including because chances are good you've eaten their bread on multiple occasions at your favorite restaurant. From baguettes to pretzel rolls to *ciabatta* to cranberry walnut bread, Slow Dough's Heath Wendell, a fifth-generation baker, is making some of the best breads in town. Find his products at various farmers' markets, **Revival Market** (see p. 85), or restaurants throughout town.

Spec's, 2410 Smith St., Houston, TX 77006; (713) 526-8787; www
.specsonline.com. Whether you're having a party and want to get a
keg or have simply grown tired of your favorite dinner wine, Spec's
is the place to go for all of your booze-related needs. Come on a
Saturday for samples of some Texas-based liquors, wines, and beers
and grocery items such as cheeses, chocolates, and breads—there's
also a full gourmet grocery section of the store. There are multiple
Spec's locations in Houston, although this location has the widest
variety of products. Pay with cash or debit card and get an extra
discount.

Sprinkles Cupcakes, 4014 Westheimer Rd., Houston, TX 77027;
(713) 871-9929; www.sprinkles.com. Houstonians who had traveled
to the original Sprinkles locations in California were very excited
when news broke a few years ago that this popular cupcake shop
was making its way to Houston. And well they should have been.
Sprinkles serves up some of the most delicious—and consistent—
minicakes around. Located in the prime Highland Village shopping
area, Sprinkles regularly features flavors such as banana, chocolate
marshmallow, ginger lemon, peanut butter chip, pumpkin, vegan
red velvet, vanilla, and even doggie cupcakes (for Fido, of course).
And if you "friend" Sprinkles on Facebook, you'll be privy to deals,
specials, and insider information.

Sugarbaby's Cupcake Boutique, 3310 S. Shepherd St., Houston,
TX 77098; (713) 527-8427; www.ilovesugarbabys.com. Craving a
cupcake but want to avoid the chains that have arrived in Houston

in force in recent years? Try Sugarbaby's Cupcake Boutique, a locally owned shop that claims that by walking in the door you can "taste laughter and smell dreams." That may be a little bit of an overstatement, but the place is most certainly adorable, from the pastel-topped confections that line the long glass case to the pink and black decor that would delight any 5-year-old. Sugarbaby's also accepts orders in advance for special occasions—I ordered two dozen mini cupcakes with fondant onesies on the top for a recent baby shower and they were absolutely perfect. The flavors here can be hit-or-miss, though, so be sure to try a few to determine your favorite. Open 9 a.m. to 7 p.m. (or until they sell out) Tues through Sat.

Three Brothers Bakery, 4036 S. Braeswood Blvd., Houston, TX 77025; (713) 666-2551; www.3brothersbakery.com. Among the most famous bakeries in Houston, Three Brothers is a sweets lover's dream, with goodies to keep you on a sugar high for the rest of the year. The most popular products here include custom-made cakes, breads, bagels, gingerbread men, cookies, cupcakes, coffee cakes, pies, Danishes, and rolls. With 60 years of service under its belt, Three Brothers has definitely developed the recipe for success with friendly service, a convenient location, and, most important, delicious goods that will have you eagerly awaiting your next visit.

Urban Harvest Farmers' Market at Discovery Green, 1500 McKinney St. at Discovery Green, Houston, TX 77010; (713) 880-5540; www.urbanharvest.org. If you're looking for a fun way to fill your Sunday afternoon, head to Discovery Green, where dozens of vendors are waiting to greet you with fresh tomatoes, handmade cheese, and fresh-baked cookies. Once you're finished strolling their booths, take a walk through the other parts of Discovery Green, where you're likely to see anything from a free concert to an exercise class to happy families playing Frisbee in the grass. The market is held every Sun from noon to 4 p.m., rain or shine.

Urban Harvest Farmers' Market at Eastside, 3000 Richmond, Houston, TX 77098; (713) 880-5540; www.urbanharvest.org. Vendors here offer quite an impressive variety of goods, ranging from seafood and meat to veggies and fruits. You can also occasionally find special items and events such as fruit trees, gardening classes, and live music. This is another favorite spot of Houston chefs, who like to congregate here. The market is held every Sat from 8 a.m. to noon, rain or shine.

Whole Foods Market, 701 Waugh Dr., Houston, TX 77019; (713) 284-1260; http://wholefoodsmarket.com/stores/montrose. Yes, I know this Austin-based chain may now be found across the country, but this particular store, which opened in the summer of 2011, immediately excited Houston foodies thanks to its innovative layout. Located in the always trendy Montrose neighborhood,

this particular store features one of the first wine bars constructed inside a Whole Foods Market as well as its own smoke house (brisket, ribs, and sausage, anyone?), a made-to-order taco bar, a sprawling bakery, and a dedicated sports section within the store. When you go, expect to be instantly enticed and overwhelmed—in a good way: The store spans 45,000 square feet. Don't miss the huge beer selection, the wide selection of locally grown and sourced projects, or (my favorite) the artwork by local artists displayed throughout the store. Feeling a little tired? Hit up the Allegro Espresso bar for a perfect cup of java, featuring hard-to-find beans from around the world. There are even some electric car charging stations, should you need to recharge before you head out on your next adventure. There on a nice day? Grab a spot on the indoor-outdoor patio.

Food Events

Houston International Festival, downtown at 400 Rusk St., Houston, TX 77002; (713) 654-8808; www.ifest.org. With so many different cultures in Houston, it's only fitting that the city offer a yearly celebration of its diversity featuring a different country or geographical area. If you go to the Houston International Festival, or iFest, as it's known by locals, expect fun, song, dance, education, and food, of course. Each year the festival, which is held in April, incorporates events, history, and traditions from a different place. Past themes have included the Caribbean, the Silk Road, and Australia. The best part? Many of the festival's events are food-focused, from vendors specializing in the featured country's cuisine to cooking classes to samples of the area's hot dishes. Come hungry—you won't regret it.

Houston Livestock Show and Rodeo, 8334 Fannin St., inside Reliant Park, Houston, TX 77054; (832) 667-1000; www.hlsr.com. One of Houston's most famous annual events (typically held in March), the Houston Livestock Show and Rodeo draws more than 2 million visitors a year who are eager to test out everything from the mechanical bull to the carnival midway to the dozens and dozens of food offerings. Trust me: From the fried alligator on a stick to the funnel cakes to the Rodeo Barbecue Cook Off, the food here alone is worth the trip. You have to be invited to attend the Rodeo Barbecue Cook Off, but if you can score a ticket, you'll get your fill of free food and booze. Didn't get an invite? Don't worry. General-admission rodeo tickets start around $18.

Houston Restaurant Week, various restaurants around Houston; www.houstonrestaurantweek.com. Houston Restaurant Week actually runs for almost a month and is held twice a year around March and August, meaning you have many opportunities to get involved. Here's how it works: More than 100 of the city's best restaurants offer special menus and wonderful discounts to get you in the door.

It's a wonderful way to sample some new places and to get a good feel for what's currently trending within the city's culinary scene. Just check the online lineup and start making your plans—you've got a lot of eating to do.

Houston "Where the Chefs Eat" Culinary Tours, various locations around Houston; (713) 437-5275; www.visithoustontexas .com/culinarytours. Hosted by the Greater Houston Convention and Visitors Bureau, these culinary tours quickly made a splash thanks to their innovative concept: Famous local chefs take tour participants to their favorite area dives. The mission of the tours is simple—to introduce local residents and visitors to the diversity of Houston's culinary scene, from undiscovered restaurants to under-explored neighborhoods. The tours, which are limited to 16 participants, cost $180 a person, which includes tastings at each stop, free Saint Arnold's beverages, limo-bus transportation, and a gift bag. Ticket proceeds benefit the Houston Food Bank. Past tour themes have included Vietnamese with Ryan Pera and Bryan Caswell; pig with Chris Shepherd, Richard Knight,  and James Silk; world barbecue with Chris Shepherd and Robb Walsh; Southern comfort with Randy Evans, Mark Holley, and Rebecca Masson; the Americas with Hugo Ortega and Robb Walsh; Middle Eastern cuisine with Monica Pope, Jonathan Jones, and Hugo Ortega; and street food with Chris Shepherd and Jonathan Jones.

All tours depart from Central Market, 3815 Westheimer Rd., at 11 a.m. and return at 4 p.m. Buses will be parked in the Central Market lot with Houston Culinary Tours signage. Be sure to dress comfortably and to wear walking shoes.

Cocktail Culture

Anvil Bar and Refuge, 1424 Westheimer Rd., Houston, TX 77006; (713) 523-1622; www.anvilhouston.com. If you're trying hard to find a classic cocktail such as a Singapore Sling or simply trying to mix up your Saturday night beverage regimen, Anvil is the perfect place to go. Run by three "cocktail freaks"—Bobby Heugel, Kevin Floyd, and Steve Flippo—Anvil specializes in spirit-forward drinks that incorporate local ingredients and house-made syrups and liqueurs. The bar also serves more than a dozen difficult-to-find draft beers. Among the drink offerings: the Antebellum Julep (Demerara and Jamaica rum, molasses, sassafras, okra seed, Angostura Bitters, and mint), the Bayou Horchata (*reposado* tequila, popcorn rice, pecan, allspice dram), and the Devil's Run (sloe gin, house chicory coffee liqueur, blanc vermouth, fernet, hopped grapefruit bitters). Trust me—you won't find more innovative cocktails in town. Oh, and if you get hungry, there's a menu of small bites, frequently put together by a notable local chef.

Beaver's, 2310 Decatur St., Houston, TX 77007; (713) 864-2328; www.beavershouston.com. It's worth coming to Beaver's solely for the food, which offers a fun, innovative take on traditional barbecue in Texas. But if the summer sun has you hankering for a cocktail, Beaver's can definitely quench your thirst, with refreshing drinks you won't soon forget. Among my favorites: the Yellow Daisy (Siembra Azul organic tequila, yellow chartreuse, fresh lime juice, orange blossom water), the Belt Strap (Cruzan Black Strap rum, Southern Star Pine Belt Ale, sugar, fresh lemon juice), the Forecast (habañero-infused vodka, muddle cucumber, Kaffir lime syrup, fresh lemon juice), and the Beaver Mary (Luksusowa vodka and tomato juice infused with bruised celery, garlic, wasabi, and Big Daddy's Hot Sauce). The beer list here is also impressive, with Texas offerings such as Real Ale Brewing Co.'s Rio Blanco Pale Ale, Independence Brewing Co.'s Convict Hill Oatmeal Stout, and Southern Star Brewery's Buried Hatchet Stout.

Block 7 Wine Company, 720 Shepherd Dr., Houston, TX 77007; (713) 572-2565; www.block7wineco.com. If you love wine, you're going to enjoy a trip to Block 7 Wine Company, a retail wine and tasting room located in the bustling Washington Avenue corridor. With a large, climate-controlled wine cellar and a variety of events such as daily happy hour, salsa dancing lessons, and live music on Sunday, this is a great place to spend an afternoon learning about wine. Want a more in-depth education? Visit Block 7 on a Tuesday, when educationally driven tastings are offered from 6 to 9 p.m. Can't find anything you like? The staff will hunt it down for you. There's also a food menu that includes crispy bacon and onion flatbread; a decadent *croque-madame* sandwich; cheese plates with a variety of options; and fantastic desserts such as warm bread pudding, molten chocolate cake, and strawberry shortcake topped with whipped cream.

Cha Champagne and Wine Bar, 810 Waugh Dr., Ste. 100, Houston, TX 77019; (713) 807-0967; www.chahouston.com. Like Champagne? Then you'll love this Champagne bar, which features a gorgeous view of the downtown Houston skyline and a variety of hard-to-find Champagnes and sparkling wines, such as Nicolas Feuillatte Brut, Perrier-Jouët Grand Brut, and Barth René Cremant d'Alsace. There's also a full selection of wine and beer and a food menu with items such as flatbread pizza; a caviar trio; *foie gras* terrine; and a meat plate with mustard, olives, and cornichons. Cha also serves Champagne cocktails in flavors such as baked apple, lavender spice, and aromatic herb. Expect a variety of regular events here, such as happy hour, live music, and a DJ.

Saint Arnold Brewing Company, 2000 Lyons Ave., Houston, TX 77020; (713) 686-9494; www.saintarnold.com. Oh, Saint Arnold, how do I love thee? Let me count the ways. Texas's oldest craft brewery, Saint Arnold is a favorite among locals for a variety of reasons. First, they offer wonderful Saturday and weekday tours that include an inside view of the brewery and tastings of the 10

beers the brewery regularly produces (5 are made year-round, and 5 are seasonal). Options range from a hoppy India pale ale (Saint Arnold Elissa) to a full-bodied, chocolaty stout (Saint Arnold Winter Stout). Kids are welcome at all tours and are encouraged to taste the vibrant, nonalcoholic Saint Arnold Root Beer. Tours are held between 11 a.m. and 2 p.m. Sat and at 3 p.m. on weekdays. Afraid you'll get hungry? Pack a lunch. Food is welcome here as well.

The Tasting Room–Uptown Park, 1101 Uptown Park Blvd., Houston, TX 77056; (713) 993-9800; www.tastingroomwines.com. With 7,600 square feet of more than 200 wines, you know you're going to find something here that suits you, particularly since the price of bottles ranges from $15 to more than $1,000. You can also try dozens of wines by the glass or enjoy tastings every Saturday from 2 to 5 p.m. for $6 (buy a bottle and get your $6 back). This location also frequently offers special events such as live music, Sunday brunch, and paella tastings. Additional locations can be found at River Oaks, 2409 W. Alabama St., and CityCentre, 818 Town and Country Blvd., Ste. 100.

North Houston: The Woodlands, Spring, Conroe, Tomball & Humble

As you drive north on I-45, you will instantly notice the mix of glossy, high-end suburban shopping malls and down-home, backwoods dives. At first it probably seems like an odd mix, but what it really means is that this is a great place to go to eat.

If you want an upscale dining experience, look no farther than The Woodlands, where some of the greatest restaurants in Houston reside. Slip into your little black dress and your finest pair of Manolo Blahniks—it's all reservations and fine cocktails here.

But if you want some genuine country cooking, you won't have to go far for that, either. Just head to the small towns of Old Town

Spring, Humble, or Conroe and do some digging. Here's a tip: Even if it looks like a questionable place, if there are a lot of cars in the parking lot, that's probably a good sign that it's a solid place to go. Think chicken-fried steak, hush puppies, and fried catfish at these types of establishments.

Either way you go—upscale or down-home—you won't go wrong with a food escape to north Houston. Just try to avoid traveling during rush hour, when traffic on I-45 can slow to a snail's pace.

Foodie Faves

Black Walnut Cafe, 2520 Research Forest Dr., The Woodlands, TX 77381; (281) 362-1678; www.blackwalnutcafe.com; American; $$. With its cool light fixtures, dark, wooden furniture, and spacious patio, Black Walnut Cafe is instantly inviting. But the real reason to come here, of course, is the menu, which spans the globe with delicious dishes such as boneless buffalo-wing tacos, crab-stuffed mushrooms, potato bacon soup, build-your-own omelets, and chipotle chicken pepper pasta. Signature items include a sirloin steak dinner (10 ounces of grilled certified Angus beef with potatoes, broccoli, and garlic bread); Kirby's pot roast stew; and, my favorite, the salmon fillet, which comes with perfectly seasoned orzo, walnuts, and garlic bread. There's also a full breakfast menu that includes 3 types of eggs Benedict, pancakes, waffles, eggs, burritos, and made-to-order kolaches. Craving something sweet? There's a wide selection of cakes, pies, and gelato—take a piece of cake for the road. Three other area locations are also available.

Brickhouse Tavern, 12910 Northwest Fwy., Houston, TX 77040; (713) 462-0576; www.brickhousetavernandtap.com; American; $$. I'm embarrassed to say that I have spent countless hours at this establishment, which initially comes off as only a half step classier than Hooters. After all, there are TVs at nearly every booth and midriff-baring young waitresses in the requisite short-shorts at every turn. No matter. The drinks are strong, the service is friendly, and the food is delicious. Start with the soft pretzels (served with 3 options of dipping sauces), then move on to an entree such as tavern fish and chips, Drunken Chops, the 1.5-pound "super beast" burger, or a Double Your Pleasure BLT. You won't be disappointed by the food, or the atmosphere, actually.

Chez Roux, 600 La Torretta Blvd., Montgomery, TX 77356; (936) 448-4400; www.latorrettalakeresort.com; French; $$$$. My relationship with Chez Roux has been tumultuous, mostly because the first time I ever visited, I was turned away for wearing shorts. I was staying at La Torretta Lake Resort and Spa, and headed over to grab a bite (the restaurant is on resort property) after lounging at the pool. Big mistake. Chez Roux is not that kind of place. In fact, this lakeside spot by Chef Albert Roux is downright fancy, with a wide contemporary French menu that pays special attention to fresh and locally sourced ingredients. It

took me awhile to get over the sting of being turned away, but I finally went back—and I'm glad I did. The items here, from Gulf shrimp over couscous to wild boar to Duck Tourte, were perfection, as was the wine list. Just be sure you leave your shorts at home.

Chuy's Comida Deluxe, 19827 Northwest Fwy., Jersey Village, TX 77065; (281) 970-0341; www.chuys.com; Tex-Mex; $$. Originally founded in Austin in 1982, this local chain has expanded to include locations around the state. Known for its kitschy decor (Elvis has a special place at each and every one of these restaurants) and fantastic, fresh Tex-Mex, Chuy's Comida Deluxe is among the best restaurants offering south of the border fare in Houston. Don't miss the "big as yo' face burritos" or the excellent salads, particularly the Mexi-Cobb salad, which is filled with flavorful chicken, cheese, and chiles. All tortillas here are hand rolled and all salsa is made fresh every hour. Green chiles are also featured prominently throughout the menu, popping up in everything from ranchero salsa to a special menu featured annually during green chile season. The drinks here, particularly the Mexican martini, are also fantastic. Five additional locations are in the Houston area.

Egg Cetera Breakfast and Lunch Cafe, 3010 W. Davis St., Conroe, TX 77304; (936) 539-3447; Breakfast; $. Don't let the name deceive you. The offerings here include much more than just breakfast fare, such as house-made chips and salsa, Tex-Mex dishes, tamales, tortilla soup, and

more. But if you're craving breakfast, you won't be disappointed, with dishes that include egg skillets (expect a big jumble of goodies such as steak, potatoes, and onions), omelets, pancakes, waffles, huevos rancheros, and more. It's open only until 2 p.m. daily, however, so be sure you get there early.

Grotto, 9595 Six Pines, Ste. 100, The Woodlands, TX 77380; (281) 419-4252; www.grottohouston.com; Italian; $$. You love Italian food but you don't want to go to Romano's Macaroni Grill or the Olive Garden. Here's a perfect alternative: Grotto. This Italian trattoria is warm and inviting with an instant Tuscan vibe. And the food is a can't-miss. Think decadent appetizers such as calamari *toto* (fried calamari in marinara), crab claws *scapricciatiello,* and chicken cannelloni. For entrees, get ready for linguine *pescatore* (linguine with shrimp, calamari, mussels, clams, and crab claws with herbs and white wine tomato sauce), veal *kickerillo* (Parmesan-crusted scaloppini with mushrooms and a touch of lemon), and grilled snapper *ceretto* (portobello mushrooms, shrimp, and tomatoes in Pinot Grigio sauce). There's also brunch, a full line of desserts, and hundreds of wines from Italy.

Humble City Cafe, 200 E. Main St., Humble, TX 77338; (281) 319-0200; www.humblecitycafe.com; Southern; $$. If you don't live in Humble, you may not end up that way very often, but here's a destination that makes the 30-minute drive from downtown well worth it: Humble City Cafe. Filled with all the charm you'd expect from a small-town cafe, Humble City dishes up some of the greatest

Southern specialties around. If you go at lunch, grab a standout sandwich, such as a traditional Reuben, a kicked-up Cajun chicken sandwich, or stuffed po'boy. For dinner, get ready for scrumptious chicken-fried steak (can be ordered half or whole); chicken-fried chicken; 12-ounce rib eye; pork chops; and plenty of sides that include fried okra, sautéed cabbage, grilled zucchini, stewed apples, and glazed carrots. There's also a large selection of salads (my favorite is the buffalo chicken) and special menus for seniors and kids.

Jasper's, 9595 Six Pines, Ste. 900, The Woodlands, TX 77380; (281) 298-6600; www.kentrathbun.com/jaspers; Southern; $$$. I was first introduced to Jasper's during happy hour, which runs daily from 3 to 7 p.m., when the food specials are so good that it's hard to resist ordering the full menu. Items such as herb-fried goat cheese with crostini and *carne guisada* flautas are just $5 during happy hour. To go with it, there's a $5 drink menu with offerings such as Dirty Blue Martinis. Want a great dinner instead? Choose from corn-crusted black drum, Texas peach barbecued pork tenderloin, and steaks that range in cut from filet to rib eye to strip, covered in your choice of glaze and served with a potato and veggie. Breakfast and lunch are also served here, and the outside patio is perfect for people watching.

Lupe Tortilla Mexican Restaurant, 15315 North Fwy., Houston, TX 77090; (281) 873-6220; www.lupetortilla.com; Tex-Mex; $$. Originally I fell in love with Lupe Tortilla for its quesadillas.

Brimming with cheese and perfectly cooked strips of fajita chicken and wrapped in a melt-in-your-mouth homemade tortilla, it was Tex-Mex perfection. Slather on a little salsa and guacamole and you won't be hungry for the rest of the day. Soon I became enamored with Lupe Tortilla's other charms: strawberry margaritas, a killer patio, tangy salsa, and sizzling fajitas. Basically you can't go wrong when you come here. Some of the locations even have playgrounds for the kids. You may have to wait if you come on a weekend evening, but it's worth it. Just grab a margarita or a beer at the bar and relax—you're in for a treat. There are multiple other Lupe Tortilla locations in Houston.

Kirby's Prime Steakhouse, 1111 Timberloch Place, The Woodlands, TX 77380; (281) 362-1121; http://kirbyssteakhouse .com; Steak House; $$$$. Texas is known for its steak houses, so it makes sense that visitors to The Woodlands would want to put Kirby's on their list of to-try places. One of three locations in the state and the only one near Houston, Kirby's offers a mouthwatering selection of steaks that includes a 22-ounce rib eye, a 30-ounce porterhouse, a 10-ounce pepper steak, a 14-ounce Australian rack of lamb, a 14-ounce veal chop, and a tenderloin tips trio. Sides include grilled rosemary zucchini, Susie's Famous Mashed Potatoes, fresh sautéed spinach, mac and cheese, and lobster risotto. A variety of seafood dishes and desserts are also available, and live music is offered Thurs through Sat.

Viking Cooking School

Always wanted to learn to cook, and cook well? Located on the second floor of Hubbell & Hudson (24 Waterway Ct.; 281-203-5650; www.vikingcookingschool.com), the **Viking Cooking School** lets you pick and choose from a variety of entertaining classes. Sign up with your sweetie, your child, or simply by yourself—you'll have a great time here. Classes range from movie-inspired sessions (think *Julie & Julia* come to life) to ethnic cuisine (a "Teens Latin Sizzle" course based on cooking from Mexico, Spain, and Argentina was recently featured) and basics such as knife skills. Times, class lengths, and prices vary; call for details.

Nit Noi Thai, 6700 Woodlands Pkwy., Ste. 250, The Woodlands, TX 77382; (281) 367-3355; www.nitnoithai.com; Thai; $$. With such a fantastic mix of cultures in Houston, Thai food has always been popular. And if you need to get your Thai fix, there's no better place than Nit Noi Thai, which has multiple locations in the Houston area. I like The Woodlands location for its laid-back vibe and its wide, Chinese-meets-Thai menu, which includes ample appetizers (satay, shrimp toast, stir-fried chicken lettuce wrap); soups (hot and sour, egg-drop, Thai noodle, wonton); noodles (including rice, clear, and deep-fried egg); salads (such as noodle, beef, and squid); and entrees that include Thai-style egg foo yong, chicken curry, pork *pan-aeng*, beef with sweet basil and hot peppers, shrimp with garlic and vegetables, and stir-fried Thai eggplant with garlic sauce.

Puffabellys Restaurant, 100 Main St., Spring, TX 77373; (281) 350-3376; www.puffabellys.com; Southern; $$. I love Old Town Spring. From its charming shops to its throwback feel, it's a great place to spend a Saturday afternoon. But one of the best reasons I've found to visit is Puffabellys Restaurant, a go-to spot for Texas staples such as chicken-fried steak, fried catfish, burgers, and hush puppies. Among my favorite dishes here: Puff-A-Peppers (handmade cheese balls stuffed with jalapeños, battered and fried, and served with ranch dressing), the bacon cheese chicken burger, and the grilled lemon pepper catfish and shrimp. Enjoy your delicious food, then stay for some live music, which is featured at Puffabellys several nights a week. Open-mic night is always held on Thurs.

Strata Restaurant and Bar, 122 Vintage Park Blvd., Houston, TX 77070; (281) 379-2889; www.stratahouston.com; American; $$$. Surrounded by warm colors and a dark, rich wood, you instantly feel welcome at Strata Restaurant and Bar, where contemporary American cuisine is the order of the day. Created to offer a "strata" of flavors to visitors, the dishes here are fun and tantalizing. Don't miss the incredible happy hour deals daily from 3 to 7 p.m.; you can sit out on the wide patio and choose from select $5 cocktails and $5 "bar bites," such as habañero sausage, empanadas, escargot, bacon mac and cheese, and an Italian meat sampler. Want something a little more substantial? How about shrimp and grits, duck confit, roasted pork tenderloin, seven-spice braised short ribs, or braised lamb shank? Sides include sautéed crabmeat, grilled asparagus, corn bread pudding, sautéed mushrooms, and quinoa risotto.

Tavola Tuscan Bistro, 32623 FM 2978, Magnolia, TX 77354; (281) 252-8700; www.tavolaonline.com; Italian; $$. There are all kinds of Italian restaurants out there, but Tavola is the real deal, featuring a menu filled with recipes that have been passed down through the owner's family for decades. Dishes include Tuscan flatbread, filet Ferri (center-cut certified Angus tenderloin with rosemary whipped potatoes), veal Vincent (veal coated with Parmesan, sautéed in olive oil, and topped with artichoke hearts and lemon butter), five-cheese lasagna with homemade meat sauce, and spaghetti and homemade meatballs, of course. The restaurant also offers a fantastic Sunday brunch buffet, a wide selection of desserts, and more than 170 bottles of wine.

Tommy Bahama Restaurant & Store, 9595 Six Pines, Ste. 700, The Woodlands, TX 77380; (281) 292-8669; www.tommy bahama.com; American; $$. I always assumed the food at the Tommy Bahama Restaurant & Store would be little more than glorified Applebee's fare—after all, isn't the guy known for making shirts? But since The Woodlands is home to one of his restaurants, and there are only about a dozen in existence, I figured it was worth a try. I'm glad I went. The food was actually top-notch, with a menu serving up tropical-themed fare such as a battered fish sandwich, fish tacos, and crab cakes, as well as standards such as cheeseburgers. Your adventure starts with warm bread and butter brought to your table and a selection of drinks such as flavored mojitos, key lime martinis, and mango iced tea. They also offer live music on weekends, and outside seating.

Uni Sushi, 9595 Six Pines, Ste. 860, The Woodlands, TX 77380; (281) 298-7177; www.unisushiwoodlands.com; Japanese; $$. More than just a sushi joint, Uni Sushi offers Japanese-European fusion cuisine, with innovative dishes such as egg roll prawns, rib eye beef rolls, Chilean sea bass, *yaki udon* (that's *udon* noodles with shaved rib eye and tempura shrimp sautéed with veggies in olive oil and soy), and Firecracker Chicken. Now, let's talk sushi. If you're a sushi lover, you'll appreciate the range here, which includes baby snapper, yellowtail, arctic char, amberjack, freshwater eel, sweet shrimp, whole scallop, smelt roe, habañero-infused *tobiko,* and soft-shell crawfish. Also, don't miss the fabulous lunch plate bento boxes, which include an entree as well as steamed rice, vegetable tempura or steamed vegetables, and orzo miso soup or a fresh lunch salad with ginger vinaigrette or miso dressing. It's the perfect lunch combination.

Vernon's Kuntry Katfish, 5901 W. Davis St., Conroe, TX 77304; (936) 760-3386; www.kuntrykatfish.com; Southern; $$. Come on. If you see a place with a name like this, how can you not go in? But kitschy name aside, is the food actually good? Thankfully, yes. Very good. Started as a 10-table joint in 1984, Vernon's Kuntry Katfish is now the place to go in Conroe and the surrounding area for fried Southern goodies such as Katfish bites, onion rings, fried oysters, fried pickles, fried yellow squash, fried green tomatoes, fried cheese sticks, and Krab Kakes. (See what I was saying about the fried theme?) It's the seafood, however, that really keeps people coming back, with wonderful offerings such as famous Large Katfish with 2 sides, crawfish étouffée, shrimp creole, and blackened scallops. Sides include coleslaw, tater tots, kernel corn, rice with gravy, mashed potatoes, and stuffed baked potatoes.

Specialty Stores, Markets & Producers

Elizabeth Lachlan Pastries, meetings by appointment only at her shop in The Woodlands; (281) 795-5034; http://elizabeth lachlan.com. Planning a wedding or a birthday shower, or just want to enjoy a delicious slice of cake? Get in touch with Elizabeth Lachlan Pastries, where Amy Cotten bakes up incredible wedding, birthday, and holiday cakes as well as cupcakes, cookies, and other goodies. Orders should be placed at least 2 weeks in advance, and samples are available if you'd like to try something out. If you're hankering for a cookie, Cotten also creates a variety of shapes and sizes, from flip-flops to onesies to mermaids. Custom-designed cookies are also available.

Frost Bake Shoppe, 6777 Woodlands Pkwy., Suite 304, The Woodlands, TX 77382; (281) 298-7474; www.frostbakeshoppe.com. The motto here is "everyone deserves the sweetest things in life," and that's a sentiment I can wholeheartedly agree with. Frost Bake Shoppe prides itself on small-batch baking and quality ingredients, which results in delicious goodies such as cookies, brownies, and cupcakes. Cupcake flavors include pumpkin, cookies and cream, turtle, Italian cream, snickerdoodle, lemon, black velvet, chocolate overload, key lime, chocolate dream, confetti (a favorite of little kiddos), vanilla chocolate, and red velvet, as well as weekly specialty flavors such as snowball, chocolate-salted caramel, orange Dreamsicle, margarita, and blueberry cheesecake. My mouth is watering just thinking about it.

Hebert's Specialty Meats, 1023 Dairy Ashford, Houston, TX 77079; (281) 558-6328; www.hebertsspecialtymeats.com. You haven't lived until you've found yourself up to your elbows in a mass of poultry that includes a turkey, a duck, and a chicken.

That's right—making a turducken is basically a cook's rite of passage these days. But if that doesn't sound appealing to you, you can always go to Hebert's Specialty Meats, which offers not only turduckens but also other specialty meats and dishes such as boudin, sausage, stuffed chicken, gumbo, beef roasts, pork roasts, crawfish pies, and more. Stuffing options for the turduckens include crawfish dressing, rice dressing, shrimp dressing, and corn bread dressing. If you've never tried a turducken and don't want to cook one yourself, this is most definitely the place for you.

Hubbell & Hudson, 24 Waterway Ct., The Woodlands, TX 77380; (281) 203-5600; www.hubbellandhudson.com. Any place with an encouraged "sip and shop" policy—meaning you're encouraged to grab a glass of wine or a beer as you browse the store—is okay in my book. And this market-bistro is a great one to browse. It's like a miniature but just as satisfying Whole Foods, with everything from samples of jalapeño cheddar bread to slow-roasted potatoes ready for pick up from the deli to a floral department with offerings to rival your local florist's. Still hungry after your visit? Head next door to the Hubbell & Hudson Bistro, which uses fresh, in-season ingredients to cook up dishes such as pan-seared *foie gras* and free-range chicken breast. The bistro also has a full bar.

Veron's Cajun Meat Market, 8059 FM 1960 East, Humble, TX 77346; (281) 812-4181; www.veronsmeatmarket.com. No place (except maybe Louisiana) loves its Cajun food as much as Texas, but if you're not sure where to go for the best Cajun seasonings, meats, and other products, give Veron's a shot. Items include juicy steaks (including rib eyes, filet mignon, T-bones, porterhouses, and New York strips), deboned chicken stuffed with jalapeño corn bread, crawfish jambalaya or Cajun dirty rice, Cajun seasoning, head cheese, boudin, crabmeat-stuffed mushrooms, red beans and sausage, and fried turkey. And since the Veron family is originally from Louisiana, you know it's authentic.

The Woodlands Gourmet Bakery and Cafe, 9950 Woodlands Pkwy., The Woodlands, TX 77382; (281) 298-9684; http://thewoodlands gourmetbakery.com. If you've ever been to Paris, you may find that you periodically, randomly crave a *pain au chocolat* (aka chocolate croissant) and a delicious espresso. The Woodlands Gourmet Bakery is like being transported to Paris—minus the $700 airfare. Specialties here include perfectly flaky croissants, decadent sandwiches on fresh-baked bread, Danishes, sticky buns, lemon tarts, chocolate éclairs, quiche, paninis, and a wide selection of coffee drinks. The best part? Most of the pastries are $2 to $3. Not bad for a delicious breakfast. *Bonjour!*

Conroe Cajun Catfish Festival, downtown Conroe; www.conroe cajuncatfishfestival.com. Love catfish? Then you're going to love this lively annual celebration of food, music, and family. Created to benefit the nonprofit Friends of Conroe Inc., which works to enhance the quality of life in Conroe, the Conroe Cajun Catfish Festival features a petting zoo; children's rides; a stellar music lineup; and food such as shrimp gumbo, frog legs, alligator, boudin, sausage, chicken, red beans and rice, and plenty of catfish, of course. Held annually in mid-October.

Grogan's Mill Center Spring and Fall Farmers' Market, 25114 Grogan's Mill Rd., The Woodlands, TX 77380; www.grogans millvillage.com. There's nothing like a great farmers' market for stocking up on all of your favorite fruits, veggies, and bread, and the spring and fall markets at Grogan's Mill Center are wonderful ones to try. Vendors sell a range of goods that includes fresh ground and whole-bean coffee, homemade tamales, doggie baked goods and treats, artisan cheese from the **Houston Dairymaids** (see p. 79), antibiotic- and hormone-free beef, Indian food, sustainably grown vegetables and micro greens, handmade baking mixes, orchids and blooming plants, and olive oil and balsamic vinegar. The markets are held on Sat from 8 a.m. to noon in the Grogan's Mill Center parking lot near Randalls supermarket.

Taste of the Town, The Woodlands Waterway Marriott & Convention Center, 1601 Lake Robbins Dr., The Woodlands, TX 77380; (281) 367-5777; http://taste.woodlandschamber.net. Come ready to be dazzled by the chocolate-drizzled pastries, elegantly presented salmon, perfectly tossed salads, and aptly portioned appetizers. But even though they look like works of art, the tasting is even better, with more than 70 area restaurants represented. Tickets include food, beverages, and festivities.

Texas Crawfish & Music Festival, Old Town Spring; www.texas crawfishfestival.com. Whether you're a Texas native or you just moved here, you probably know that we Texans take our crawfish seriously. Every spring, when that celebrated season comes around, you can find us sitting outside on sun-drenched porches, swigging beer, and peeling spice-covered crawfish. So it's only fitting that the Texas Crawfish & Music Festival would be a splendid affair. Held annually in Old Town Spring over two weekends in May, the festival includes more than 25 tons of perfectly cooked crawfish, major touring acts such as Jason Allen, Roger Creager, and Cory Morrow, and carnival rides for the family.

Texas Renaissance Festival, 21778 FM 1774, Plantersville, TX 77363; (800) 458-3435; www.texrenfest.com. Can you say turkey leg? Sure, there are lots of reasons to visit the Texas Renaissance Festival, one of the country's largest festivals of its kind. Maybe you want a chance to break out that chain-mail. Or perhaps you really like watching a good joust. But if you're like me, the real reason to go is for the food, which ranges in offerings from steak on a stick to kettle corn to handmade banana-and-beef empanadas to "dragon's meat." Honestly, you have to go see for yourself to truly understand it. Held annually on weekends in Oct and Nov.

Wine and Food Week, various locations around The Woodlands; (713) 557-5732; www.wineandfoodweek.com. Held in June, this annual celebration of food and wine includes famous chefs from across the country and more than 500 wines. Expect master sommeliers, a wine walk through Market Street, panels about wine tasting, one-on-one visits with winemakers, a tasting lounge, and a Texas Monthly Chef Showcase with demonstrations, a live auction, and fresh local and sustainable foods.

Cocktail Culture

CRU, 9595 Six Pines, Ste. 650, The Woodlands, TX 77380; (281) 465-9463; www.cruwinebar.com. If you enjoy wine—as most good foodies do—you'll enjoy spending an evening at CRU, which claims to be "all about the wine." With the more than 30 wines by the glass, a 300-bottle wine list, and a variety of wine flights, you're guaranteed to find something that suits your palate here. In the mood for a nibble? Try an artisan cheese plate; appetizers such as cheese and tomato basil soup, chicken and shrimp pot stickers, or stone-fired pizza; or entrees such as fettuccini, grilled salmon, or seared sea scallops. Sunday brunch is also available.

Crush Wine Lounge, 20 Waterway Ct., The Woodlands, TX 77380; (281) 362-7874; www.thecrushbar.com. **Sexy.** That's really the best word to describe this cool lounge with a sprawling rooftop patio and a selection of hundreds of wines, including hard-to-find boutique varieties and up-and-comers. Mixed drinks are also available. Hungry? Try house-marinated olives, beef carpaccio with sautéed capers, truffled forest wild mushroom flat-bread pizza, Kobe beef sliders with white wine cheese fondue, or dark chocolate and white dried cherry truffles with fresh mixed berries. Between the hot customers, mouthwatering fare, and swoon-worthy wines, you might just find yourself leaving with a crush.

Goose's Acre Bistro and Irish Pub, 21 Waterway Ave., Ste. 140, The Woodlands, TX 77380; (281) 466-1502; www.the goosesacre.com. When Brian Young and Colm O'Neill heard that the Goose's Acre Irish Pub was closing in Midleton, Ireland, they did what any good Irish lads would do—they brought the bar, piece by piece, over to The Woodlands. The result is a fantastic, authentic-feeling European pub with a wide selection of cocktails, wines, and beer—including Guinness, of course. The food selection is solid as well, with options that include classics such as cod fish and chips, corned beef and cabbage, sirloin shepherd's pie, and newer options including wood-fired pizza, barbecue beef back ribs, spicy glazed shrimp, and grilled ahi tuna steak.

Southern Star Brewing Company, 1207 N. FM 3083 East, Conroe, TX 77303; (936) 441-2739; www.southernstarbrewery.com.
 This craft beer house radiates cool, from its attractively designed beer cans to the free tours—and ample tastings—it offers at the 10,000-square-foot brewery most Saturdays. Just arrive at 1 p.m. and take the tour, then get tastings of Southern Star favorites such as Buried Hatchet stout, Bombshell Blonde ale, and Pine Belt pale ale. Tours are always free; no reservations are required. Kids are welcome as long as they are supervised.

WineStyles The Vintage, 10300 Louetta Rd., Ste. 150, Houston, TX 77070; (281) 257-9463; www.winestyles.net/louetta. At first it's difficult to understand the concept of this neat little space. After all, it's part gift shop, part wine shop, and part tasting room. But if you're a food lover, you'll be impressed by the selection here, which includes a variety of wines for under $30 a bottle. You can also join the wine club for additional discounts. If you get hungry, grab a spot on the patio, where cheese plates, pizza, and other dishes are available. Sometimes you'll also find live music here.

West Houston: Galleria, Sugar Land, Missouri City, Bellaire & CityCentre

Houston has been widely criticized for its sprawl. Heck, it was even the subject of Arcade Fire's Grammy-winning album, *The Suburbs*. But as annoying as those pockets of green attached to highways may be, they're also filled with gems. The upside, if you're a foodie living in Houston, is that you never know where you may find your next favorite meal. Stop in Sugar Land, one of the fastest-growing master-planned communities in the country, and be overwhelmed by the upscale and internationally infused offerings. Drop by CityCentre, a relatively new shopping and entertainment district, and find restaurants that run a full span, from Ruggles Green, the first Houston restaurant to be certified by the Green Restaurant Association, to Flora & Muse, a flower shop/cafe like something you might find on the streets of Paris. West Houston is absolutely brimming with places you'll want to see and return to, again and again.

Foodie Faves

Aura Restaurant, 3340 FM 1092, Ste. 160, Missouri City, TX 77459; (281) 403-2872; www.aura-restaurant.com; French; $$$. The brainchild of Frederic Perrier, a native of Lyon, France, who spent years working in some of New York City's best restaurants, Aura Restaurant offers French-infused American cuisine. Favorite menu items include a goat cheese and beet salad; crab beignets with Tabasco pulp remoulade; Michelle's Humble Fog goat cheese tart; a grilled Kurobuta pork chop; beef medallions Diane; and Frenchy's decadent burger with prime beef, braised oxtail, *foie gras,* balsamic onion compote, and *pommes frites.* Lunch is also available, as is a sunset menu served Tues through Sat from 5 to 6:30 p.m. that includes 3 courses for $24.50 and select bottles of wine for $19.99. The restaurant is closed Sun and Mon.

Azuma Sushi and Robata Bar, 15830 Southwest Fwy., Ste. 100, Sugar Land, TX 77478; (281) 313-0518; www.azumarestaurant.com; Japanese; $$. Azuma Sushi and Robata Bar is a dependable place to go for good-quality sushi in a comfortable atmosphere. Happy hour is one of the biggest draws here thanks to specials that include discounted rolls, small dishes, and sashimi. Don't miss the Crazy Irishman, the Lady Dragon Roll, the crunchy roll, or the spicy tuna roll. Yum. Additional locations are at 5600 Kirby Dr. and 909 Texas St.

Big Woodrow's, 3111 Chimney Rock Rd., Houston, TX 77056; (713) 784-2653; www.bigwoodrows.com; Southern; $$. Okay, at first glance this place may look like a standard icehouse, but once you glance over the menu you'll see that there's much more to it than football games and beer buckets (although those are both big draws). The menu is a mix of Cajun and standard bar specialties, expertly prepared. Start with an order of fried alligator, popcorn shrimp, and Texas hush puppies, followed by a Cajun-chicken Philly cheesesteak, a Texan burger (½-pound patty topped with onion rings, cheddar cheese, bacon, lettuce, tomato, and barbecue sauce), chicken and sausage jambalaya, or a huge mess of crawfish (when in season). All are stellar. Other menu standouts include the fried menu items, such as fried oysters, fried crawfish tails, a fried-shrimp basket, fried pickles, fried mushrooms, fried zucchini sticks, fried mozzarella, fried okra . . . You get the idea. Live music is also regularly featured. Grab a group of friends and plan to spend an afternoon here—once you arrive here you're not going to want to leave for a while.

Bistro Alex, 800 W. Sam Houston Pkwy. North, Houston, TX 77042; (713) 827-3545; www.bistroalex.com; French; $$. Located in the sparkling CityCentre complex, this little brother to **Brennan's** (see p. 69) offers fantastic French-American bistro cuisine in a comfortable, cozy atmosphere. Expect menu items such as Brennan's turtle soup, confit rabbit salad, a "duck debris" and butternut waffle appetizer, scallops and crawfish, blackened Maple Leaf Farm duck breast, and 3-course packages for $38. Side dishes include oven-roasted vegetables, olive-oil wilted spinach, goat cheese grits, and *pommes frites*. Breakfast, lunch, and brunch menus are also available. And don't miss the adjacent Bistro Bar, which is filled with innovative cocktails and interesting appetizers in a sexy atmosphere.

Blue Nile Ethiopian Restaurant, 9400 Richmond Ave., Houston, TX 77063; (713) 782-6882; www.bluenilerestaurant.com; Ethiopian; $$. I spent several years trying to find good Ethiopian food in Houston, so I was delighted when at long last I discovered Blue Nile. The restaurant, which opened in 1994, is known both for its food and for its authentic *injera* bread, which can be extremely

hard to come by in Houston. Menu items here include all of your favorites, such as mixed vegetables with garlic, ginger, turmeric, and olive oil; red lentil stew; lamb cubes in a mix of spices; minced beef in Ethiopian spices; grilled chicken breast; and fresh shrimp. As is the case at most Ethiopian restaurants, the best way to try it out is to visit with friends and order up one of the hearty combinations. Scared of eating with your hands in front of a group? Don't be. That's the way it's done here.

Brio Tuscan Grille, 12808 Queensbury Ln., Ste. 100, Houston, TX 77024; (713) 973-9610; www.brioitalian.com; Italian; $$. Yes, you might see couples on their way to prom (as we did during one of our visits) or a big group of family members celebrating a milestone occasion, and why not? With its elegant-yet-not-too-fancy vibe and top-notch cuisine, I wouldn't mind celebrating my birthday at Brio, either. This chain features wonderful homemade bread and an impressive selection of bruschetta that includes varieties such as shrimp and chorizo, sliced steak, roasted red pepper and fresh mozzarella, and classic tomato. Menu favorites include Tuscan grilled pork chops, sweet potato and chicken risotto, lobster ravioli with crab *insalata*, veal Milanese, and artichoke-crusted beef medallions. There's also a weekend brunch (think white chocolate raspberry french toast, crab and shrimp crepes, and grilled chicken and chorizo Benedict), happy hour specials, and a fantastic dessert menu.

Brookstreet Barbecue, 1418 Highway 6, Sugar Land, TX 77478; (281) 313-4000; www.brookstreetbbq.com; Barbecue; $$. Despite

Houston's well-known food scene and abundance of great restaurants, finding good barbecue can be hit-or-miss. But this barbecue joint, which prides itself on selling authentic Texas barbecue at low prices, tends to be spot on. The menu is pretty standard: 1-, 2-, and 3-meat plates with options such as beef, sausage, pulled pork, smoked turkey, and ribs served with 2 sides; sandwiches and po'boys such as Carolina pork, pulled chicken, and turkey; hamburgers; and take-out value packs. The prices are low and the servings are generous. Additional locations may be found at 7232 Highway 6 in Missouri City and 10705 Westheimer Rd.

Burning Pear, 16090 City Walk, Sugar Land, TX 77479; (281) 275-5925; www.theburningpear.com; Southern; $$$. Located in the heart of Sugar Land's bustling Town Square, the Burning Pear is a wonderful place to try if you're in the mood for Texas regional cuisine. Menu items here include a mix of Southern classics such as catfish cakes, Gulf Coast gumbo, brown sugar and mustard–rubbed 16-ounce rib eye with garlic mash and green beans, chicken-fried steak, broiled redfish salad, and a variety of perfectly crafted sandwiches such as the ultimate ham and 3-cheese melt on Texas toast and the BP ½-pound burger with roasted poblano, caramelized onions, and Jack cheese. Staying at the adjacent Marriott Town Square? Drop by the Denim Bar, which is attached to the restaurant and overlooks the hotel's courtyard. Breakfast, brunch, and lunch are also served.

Candelari's Pizza, 6825 S. Fry Rd., Katy, TX 77494; (281) 395-6746; http://candelaris.com; Italian; $$. Craving pizza and trying to avoid the major chains? In Houston we're lucky to have a little place named Candelari's Pizza, which has been serving up New York–style pizza since 2003. Considered by some to be the best pizza in the city, you can expect a pie from Candelari's to have the freshest ingredients, such as buffalo mozzarella, smoked turkey jalapeño sausage, smoked chicken apple sausage, sun-dried tomatoes, black olives, green olives, Roma tomatoes, roasted red peppers, and a veggie mix. Other menu items include Mediterranean mussels, garlic bread, grilled vegetables, buffalo wings, salads, sandwiches, pasta, and entrees such as chicken Parmesan and grilled salmon. Got kiddos at home? Grab a take-'n'-make pizza kit, which comes with an uncooked ball of dough, original pizza sauce, mozzarella cheese, and 2 toppings of your choice. Additional locations are at 25680 Northwest Fwy., 6002 Washington Ave., 2617 W. Holcombe, and 14545 Memorial Dr.

Courses Restaurant, 1900 Yorktown St. at the Art Institute of Houston, Houston, TX 77056; (713) 353-3644; www.artinstitutes.edu; American; $$$. Okay, here's the cool thing about this place: Not only can you have an upscale lunch prepared by some of the country's brightest up-and-coming culinary stars, but you can also

THE STARS AT NIGHT ARE BIG AND BRIGHT

Every town has its share of local celebrity chefs, people who make the culinary scene brighter with their unique takes on classic cuisine. But in Houston we're fortunate to have several legitimate celebrities who have been featured all over the world, everywhere from *Gourmet* magazine to the Food Network.

Here are three names to know:

Bryan Caswell: The owner of **Reef** (see p. 51), **Little Bigs** (see p. 39), and **El Real Tex-Mex Cafe** has also become a fixture on the Food Network, appearing in shows such as *The Next Iron Chef* and *Best in Smoke*. He was also a James Beard Award semifinalist and was listed as one of *Food & Wine's* best new chefs in 2009.

Monica Pope: Chef Monica Pope has long been lauded as one of Houston's hottest chefs, with a number of awards, including a James Beard Award nomination, under her belt. But it wasn't until she competed on the second season of Bravo's *Top Chef Masters* in 2010 that she really gained national fame. A visit to her restaurant, **T'Afia** (see p. 60), is considered a must for any Houston food lover.

Jonathan Jones: Formerly chef at **Max's Wine Dive** (see p. 41) and now executive chef at **Beaver's** (see p. 4), Jonathan Jones for years has been a fixture in the Houston food community. Last spring the fruits of his labor—namely a pulled pork sandwich with three-seed slaw—were featured on the new Food Network series *Meat & Potatoes*.

do it for really cheap—roughly half the price of what you'd pay in a fine restaurant. That's because these rising stars are students at the Art Institute of Houston who prepare these meals under the direction of chef instructors. Expect dishes such as gumbo, grilled salmon, roasted chicken, and flat iron steak. The restaurant is open from 11 a.m. to 1 p.m. Mon through Thurs; make reservations in advance.

Cyclone Anaya's Mexican Kitchen, 5761 Woodway Dr., Houston, TX 77057; (713) 339-4552; www.cycloneanayas.com; Tex-Mex; $$. Named for a professional wrestler, Cyclone Anaya's Mexican Kitchen has quickly become a local favorite for anyone trying to get their Tex-Mex fix. The menu here is a bit more upscale than you might find elsewhere—offerings include roasted duck empanadas, grilled salmon salad, tamarind-braised beef short ribs, and slow-roasted *carnitas* with black-bean creamed corn, cilantro rice, fresh salsa *verde,* and a spicy watermelon jicama salad. The dishes here can be a bit more expensive because of the hard-to-find ingredients, but the quality of the food is always top-notch. I like the lobster enchiladas, which are filled with Mexican white cheese and topped with Chardonnay cream sauce and roasted pine nuts, and the classic tacos *al carbon,* which are stuffed with beef or chicken fajita meat and served with pico de gallo, sour cream, guacamole, and shredded cheese. And don't forget to order a margarita—they're incredible. Additional locations are at 1710 Durham Dr. and 309 W. Gray St., Ste. 111.

Eddie V's Prime Seafood, 12848 Queensbury Ln., Houston, TX 77024; (832) 200-2380; www.eddiev.com; Seafood; $$$. Sure, there  are plenty of seafood restaurants in Houston, but few can come close to the freshness and innovation offered at Eddie V's Prime Seafood. It's upscale, so wear some nice duds, and be ready to spend at least $100 per couple for dinner here. Trust me, it's worth it. Among the highlights: bacon-wrapped scallops, crab cakes, seared ahi tuna, New York strip steak, Parmesan-crusted lemon sole, filet mignon, and sea bass. Oh, and don't miss the opportunity to order a side of the mac and cheese or the molten chocolate cake for dessert.

59 Diner, 10407 Katy Fwy., Houston, TX 77449; (713) 984-2500; www.59diner.com; 24-Hour Dining; $$. There are multiple locations of this famed greasy spoon (which also offers lots of healthy options as well), but I like this one because it's open 24 hours. What you'll find when you come here is a fantastic 1950s atmosphere complete with retro booths, neon signs, and lots of shakes and burgers. But there's more to this popular local joint than just a *Happy Days* vibe. There's also an impressive selection of other fare, including nearly a dozen salads (try the Third Coast Caesar—a traditional Caesar salad with loads of grilled shrimp), lighter sandwich offerings such as turkey and chicken, and a wonderful breakfast selection that includes eggs served every way you can imagine; pancakes in flavors such as blueberry, banana, pecan, chocolate chip, and strawberry; three-egg omelets; *migas;* and various breakfast platters. Craving a burger? Don't miss the Cheesebatta Bacon Burger, served with bacon, pickles, onions, mayo, American cheese, lettuce, and tomato on a grilled *ciabatta* bun. And because it's open 24 hours, you can go anytime your hunger strikes. Five additional area locations are also available; check website for hours.

Flora & Muse, 12860 Queensbury Ln., Ste. 143, Houston, TX 77024; (713) 463-6873; www.floraandmuse.com; Bistro Fare; $$. At first it can be difficult to get a read on this place, which calls itself a "European-inspired cafe, flower shop, bar, and patisserie." But once you stop trying to understand it and decide instead to simply take it in, chances are good that you're going to fall in love. Charming, intimate, and inviting all at once, Flora & Muse reminds you of that little French bistro where you had the best croissant of your life. In terms of food, expect bakery items such as fresh-baked muffins, profiteroles, and chocolate cherry bread pudding; international-inspired farm-to-table fare such as quiche Lorraine, roasted asparagus crepes, and paninis; and late-night dishes such as salmon lollipops and tikki chicken skewers. Love high tea? Head over between 2 and 5 p.m. Mon through Fri for an assortment of imported teas served with finger sandwiches and pastries.

Fung's Kitchen, 7320 Southwest Fwy., Ste. 115, Houston, TX 77074; (713) 779-2288; www.eatatfungs.com; Chinese; $$. Open daily at 11 a.m., Fung's Kitchen gives you plenty of opportunity to sample its authentic Chinese seafood dishes. All of the seafood is fresh and imported from around the world: egg crab from Australia, green mussels from New Zealand, Atlantic lobster, and live tilapia. Any time is a good time to visit, but the dim sum offerings—which include broccoli with oyster sauce, bean curd shrimp roll, steamed shrimp roll with sticky rice, and fried salty Chinese bread—are particularly popular. Other menu standouts include Peking duck, black pepper beef, and rice noodles with shrimp. Be warned, however, that if you go on the weekend, the restaurant gets particularly crowded between 11:30 a.m. and 1 p.m. It can be a bit more expensive than other similar restaurants, but it's worth the money.

HK Dim Sum, 9889 Bellaire Blvd., Houston, TX 77036; (713) 777-7029; www.hkdimsumcity.com; Chinese; $$. This is another Houston restaurant famous for its dim sum, which some Houston foodies will have you believe is the best in Houston. I can't commit to that, but I can tell you it's delicious. And unlike many of the other dim sum joints in town, the restaurant space is intimate and cozy, making for a very pleasant dining atmosphere. The restaurant opens weekdays at 10 a.m. and weekends at 9 a.m., so you have plenty of time to stop in. And trust me, you'll want to. Menu highlights include barbecue pork buns, chicken feet, fried taro, fried pork dumplings, pork ribs, shrimp puff, red bean sesame balls, and shrimp-stuffed eggplant. Another cool thing? Unlike the lunch-specific dim sum offerings at other restaurants, you can have dim sum any time of day.

Ichiban Sushi & Tapioca, 16200 Kensington Dr., Ste. 300, Sugar Land, TX 77478; (281) 265-1669; www.ichibansweethouse.com; Japanese; $$. The offerings here include a smorgasbord of items that include Japanese specialties, sushi, fresh sashimi, and goodies such as tapioca drinks and ice cream cakes. Don't expect anything fancy—the space here is very small—but the food is top-notch. Try the beef teriyaki, spider crab, fried tuna rolls, and sashimi. There are also bento boxes offered at lunch that include miso soup, salad, a main dish such as chicken teriyaki, and multiple rolls for $7.95. Open every day except Mon.

India's Restaurant, 5704 Richmond Ave., Houston, TX 77057; (713) 266-0131; www.indiasrestauranthouston.com; Indian; $$. Between the daily lunch buffet from 11 a.m. to 2:30 p.m. and dinner service starting daily at 5 p.m., you can find something to satisfy your Indian cravings here nearly any time of day. If you're going to try the buffet, be sure to go hungry: The offerings include 19 hot and cold items such as fresh-baked naan, tandoori chicken, lamb, skewered meats, and vegetarian options. For dinner expect all of the classics, such as samosas, *aloo ghobi* masala, *daal,* prawn curry, chicken tikka masala, and lamb vindaloo—all of which are excellent. Also, don't miss the garlic naan. This is arguably the best Indian restaurant in Houston.

Kim Son, 12750 Southwest Fwy., Stafford, TX 77477; (281) 575-0140; www.kimson.com; Vietnamese; $$. Kim Son has long been considered by many to be Houston's best Vietnamese restaurant, and for good reason. The food here can't be beat. It ranges from traditional appetizers such as Cornish hen and sweet sticky rice to fried chicken wings in garlic butter sauce to Chinese standards such as egg drop soup, roasted pork wontons, and egg foo yong. But one absolute must as a Houston resident or visitor is to come here for dim sum, which is served on Saturday and Sunday and offers a wide variety of Vietnamese and Chinese dishes that are wheeled by on carts. Just try to go early, around 11:30, or the wait can be long and the offerings can become sparse. Expect to get a clipboard and mark your dishes—from fried dumplings and chicken feet to pork ribs and escargot—as you go. Be sure to come hungry. Additional locations may be found at 10603 Bellaire Blvd., Ste. B2000, and 2001 Jefferson St. in Houston.

Ocean Palace Restaurant, 11215 Bellaire Blvd., Ste. D01, Houston, TX 77072; (281) 988-8898; Chinese; $$$. Yet another wonderful place to go for dim sum, Ocean Palace is a favorite among locals who pack the dining room on weekend mornings. Get ready for lots of food carts with items such as shrimp dumplings, steamed beef tripe, pork spare ribs, and barbecue pork buns, as well as food stands with hot items such as noodles and clams. Expect to pay around $30 to $40 for your meal, and to not eat for the rest of the day. Located inside Houston's bustling Chinatown district, this is by far one of the must-try spots for dim sum. They also offer a regular menu throughout the week. Once you're finished with your meal, take a walk through the adjacent shopping mall, where you never know what you'll find.

Ooh La La Dessert Boutique, 23920 Westheimer Pkwy., Katy, TX 77494; (281) 391-2253; www.oohlalasweets.com; Bakery; $$. Every time I walk into this incredible bakery, I am overwhelmed by the delicious options, which include cupcakes, cupcake towers, pies, cakes, cheesecakes, pastries, cookies, dessert bars, and custom orders. The thing I like best about the offerings here? They taste as good as they look. I am especially partial to the cupcakes, which include flavors such as Pretty in Pink (strawberry cake with cream cheese icing and pink sprinkles), Birthday Cake (vanilla cake with chocolate icing, confetti sprinkles, and candles), Boston cream pie (vanilla cake with pastry cream center, topped with chocolate ganache), and the Ultimate Chocolate Cupcake (chocolate cake with chocolate chunks, filled with chocolate ganache and topped with chocolate buttercream and chocolate chips). Daily flavors vary but include peanut butter cup, cherry limeade, piña colada, and cookies and cream. A second location is at 20155 Park Row in Katy. For Owner–Pastry Chef Vanessa O'Donnell's recipe for **chocolate chip cookies,** see p. 202.

Perry's Steakhouse & Grille, 9827 Katy Fwy., Houston, TX 77024; (832) 358-9000; www.perryssteakhouse.com; Steak House; $$$. From the swanky piano bar with live piano music on Thursday and Friday to the 20-foot climate-controlled wine tower, Perry's Steakhouse & Grill impresses with its cool, smooth ambience. Another thing that sets it apart from the upscale steak-house set in Houston: its menu. Here you'll find offerings that include an iced seafood tower, escargot, apple-wood-smoked bacon–wrapped scallops, fried asparagus, pecan-crusted red snapper, chicken Oscar, and a variety of steaks, naturally. Lunch and Sunday brunch are also offered, as is a full selection of decadent des-serts, such as deconstructed lemon meringue pie, rocky road bread pudding, white chocolate cheesecake, and flaming bananas Foster.

RA Sushi, 12860 Queensbury Ln., Ste. 234, Houston, TX 77024; (713) 331-2792; www.rasushi.com; Japanese; $$. The lighting is dim, the music is loud, and the sushi is delicious: If you're looking for a sushi experience, you've come to the right place. RA Sushi is known for both its wide selection of rolls and its stellar Japanese fusion dishes. Some of my favorite menu items include the RAllipop (tuna, salmon, yellowtail, and spicy tuna with lettuce, asparagus, and cucumber on a skewer with garlic *ponzu* sauce), RA chips and salsa (spicy tuna tartare with cucumber, avocado, and fresh salsa served with wonton chips), the ultimate shrimp tempura roll (spicy crab mixed with cucumber and shrimp tempura), and the Viva Las Vegas roll (crab and cream cheese rolled in rice and seaweed, lightly tempura battered, and topped with spicy tuna, *kanikama* crab mix, and sliced lotus root). Craving a good deal? Drop by between 3 and 7 p.m. Mon through Sat for select sushi, appetizers, and tapas ranging in price from $2 to $7. A second location is at 3908 Westheimer Rd. in Highland Village.

Ray's Grill, 8502 FM 359, Fulshear, TX 77441; (281) 533-0099; www.raysgrill.com; American; $$. Ray's Grill calls itself a "unique neighborhood bar and grill," but don't let that fool you into thinking you're going to find standard Applebee's fare here. The menu, which is dedicated to seasonal and inspired ingredients, is fantastic. And because the restaurant features a "field to table" concept, the offerings are always changing to reflect the availability of produce in the Fulshear area. Menu items include fried duck confit ravioli with fresh tomato reduction; North African spiced chicken satay with saffron tomato dipping sauce; fried white truffle mac and cheese with dried fruit chutney; chicken fried ostrich with Yukon mashed potatoes and country gravy; veal mignon with grain mustard butter, tarragon-Asiago risotto, and mild pepper natural jus; and an organic beef burger with caramelized onion and Gorgonzola cheese. Told you this wasn't Applebee's fare. Don't miss the Sunday brunch buffet, which is from 10:30 a.m. to 2 p.m., costs $20 a person, and features 99-cent mimosas. There's also live jazz every Thursday, complimentary wine tasting every Wednesday, and chef's blackboard specials from 5 p.m. to close on Tuesday and Wednesday. The restaurant is closed Mon. For Ray's Grill's recipe for **Grilled Filet Mignon Stuffed with Caramelized Onion & Maytag Blue Cheese served with Red Wine Reduction,** see p. 192.

Rudi Lechner's Restaurant and Bar, 2503 S. Gessner Rd., Houston, TX 77063; (713) 782-1180; www.rudilechners.com; German; $$. If you have even the slightest interest in anything German, you absolutely must visit Rudi Lechner's Restaurant and Bar, which has been serving up sausages, wiener schnitzel, and German beer to the masses for more than 30 years. When they say they're an authentic German restaurant, they mean it: I can't even pronounce half of what's on the menu. No matter. From incredible pork shank to roasted chicken to perfectly prepared sauerkraut, the fare here is right on. As are the special events, which range from German language classes and live German music (Wed through Sun) to special events on holidays. And obviously this is the place to come for Oktoberfest festivities, which include a German sampler buffet, live music, and drink specials. It can get crowded on weekend nights, so you may want to make a reservation.

Ruggles Green, 801 Town and Country Blvd., Ste. 1B, Houston, TX 77024; (713) 464-5557; www.rugglesgreen.com; American; $$. Any restaurant with the Ruggles name is going to be good, but Ruggles Green is special in that it is certified by the Green Restaurant Association—the first in Houston to receive this distinction—and serves organic, all-natural, hormone-free, preservative-free food. Think that means it's going to be boring and bland? Think again. Menu items include nut-crusted French brie, spicy shrimp tacos, an all-natural beef burger, an all-natural buffalo burger, a turkey meatball panini, wood-fired pizzas, spicy Southwest house-smoked chicken pasta, and desserts such as white chocolate bread pudding, Uncle Fred's high-protein hemp brownie, and pink velvet cake made with white chocolate and fresh strawberries. A second Ruggles Green is located at 2311 W. Alabama.

Straits Restaurant, 800 W. Sam Houston Pkwy. North, Ste. 940, Houston, TX 77024; (713) 365-9922; www.straitsrestaurants .com; Singaporean; $$. Aiming for an atmosphere that's chic and sleek, this chain restaurant group serves up Singaporean and Southeast Asian cuisine that can be hard to find in the United States. Standout menu items here include Indonesian corn cro-quettes, Singapore satay sticks, banana blossom salad, chicken curry potpie, and wok-fired mussels. The restaurant also serves a fantastic Singapore chile crab and black pepper crab—two Singaporean specialties that alone are worth a visit to Straits. Brunch and lunch are also served. Oh, and don't miss the weekday happy hour from 4 to 7 p.m., when wine and Champagne are $5 a glass, specialty drinks and cocktails are $6 a glass, and draft beer is $4 a glass.

Taste of Texas, 10505 Katy Fwy., Houston, TX 77024; (713) 932-6901; www.tasteoftexas.com; Steak House; $$$. Come expecting to wait. Come ready for the sprawling salad bar. And come expecting great steaks. You won't be disappointed. In a city known for its meat, Taste of Texas ranks among the best of the best. The wait can be upward of an hour on weekends, but there's free popcorn to help you kill the time—and the hunger pangs. And believe me, it's worth that wait. Let's start with the steak offerings: rib eye by the ounce, center-cut filet, slow-roasted prime rib, bone-in filet, New York strip sirloin, and a porterhouse steak for two. Other specialties include jumbo grilled shrimp, marinated steak skewer, Texas pecan-crusted chicken breast, jalapeño-stuffed shrimp, and grilled vegetable plate (which I'm willing to bet doesn't get ordered all that often, no matter how delicious it looks). Can't-miss appetizers include Texas quail bites, baked brie, and onion strings. There's also a huge wine and dessert list. Can't make it to Taste of Texas? You can have a raw steak delivered right to your front door from the restaurant's online store.

Thai Cottage, 10001 Westheimer Rd., Houston, TX 77042; (713) 266-0701; www.thai-cottage.com; Thai; $. Every now and then (or sometimes more often than that), you can't help getting a hankering for some delicious Thai food. Next time that craving strikes, head to

DINNER AND A MOVIE

No date is more classic than dinner and a movie. But if you're short on time—or dough—why not combine the two by heading to a theater that also offers a full menu? **Alamo Drafthouse** (1000 West Oaks Mall, Houston, TX 77082; 281-920-9268; www .drafthouse.com), **Studio Movie Grill** (805 Town and Country Blvd., Houston, TX 77024, and 8580 Highway 6 North, Houston, TX 77095; www.studiomoviegrill.com) and **Movie Tavern** (15719 I-45 North, Houston, TX 77090; 281-248-8397; www .movietavern.com) are among the options. When you go, expect high-class fare that may include gourmet pizzas, fine salads, and stuffed sandwiches. An added bonus? All of these places have a liquor license, meaning you can enjoy a cocktail or a beer while you eat. How's that for a good show?

Thai Cottage, which serves some of the most interesting—and delicious—Thai in the city. Simply give them a number between 1 and 5 of how spicy you'd like your meal to be and wait for the dishes to arrive. Among the best: beef satay with homemade peanut sauce and cucumber sauce; chicken fried rice; green curry chicken with coconut milk, bamboo shoots, zucchini, and basil; and vegetable pad thai with broccoli, carrots, tofu, and bean sprouts. Don't miss the luncheon special, which is offered Mon through Sat from 11 a.m. to 3 p.m. and comes with steamed rice, a vegetable crispy roll, and soup of the day or salad starting at $6.

Trattoria Il Mulino, 945 Gessner Rd., Ste. 101, Houston, TX 77024; (832) 358-0600; www.ilmulino.com/houston.html; Italian; $$$. I had my first introduction to the famed Il Mulino brand of Italian cuisine in Aspen, where the snow fell as my husband and I enjoyed some of the most flavorful Italian dishes we've ever tried. So when I heard Il Mulino was opening a smaller, more affordable branch in Houston, I figured the quality couldn't possibly live up to the reputation. I was wrong. The menu at Trattoria Il Mulino is every bit as delightful as at the other locations, with standouts that include sausage broccoli rabe with hot peppers, gnocchi Bolognese, *pollo* piccata, veal Milanese, and the famous meatballs with ricotta. There's also a $28, 3-course prix-fixe menu, as well as breakfast and lunch served every day.

Udipi Cafe, 3551 Highway 6, Sugar Land, TX 77478; (281) 313-2700; www.udipicafesugarland.com; Indian; $$. Serving only vegetarian Indian cuisine, Udipi Cafe may initially seem a little too light for the meat-eating set. But what they may lack in meat is more than made up for in taste with North and South Indian dishes that include vegetable samosas, mixed vegetable *pakoras, aloo gobi* curry, *mutter paneer, malai kofta,* and a variety of combination dishes. Don't miss the *mysore* masala *dosai*—which is like a huge crepe served with chutney, potatoes, and onions. It's a menu standout. Portions are generous and prices are moderate. A buffet is also available at certain times.

Yard House, 800 W. Sam Houston Pkwy., Houston, TX 77024; (713) 461-9273; www.yardhouse.com; American; $$. Want a cool place to go with a mixed group of guys and gals for happy hour or dinner on a Friday night? Check out the Yard House, which was founded with a goal of offering a large list of draft beer, a diverse American menu, and a wide selection of classic rock on the stereo. There are Yard House locations around the country, but ours—a relatively new one in CityCentre—is a standout. Expect to nosh on sweet potato fries with creamed maple bacon dip, *moo shu* egg rolls, sliders, a chicken enchilada stack, and lobster garlic noodles. There's also a huge list of vegetarian options that include veggie boneless wings, veggie orange-peel chicken, and veggie barbecue chicken salad. Oh, and the beer list is impressive as well, with brews that range from light summer sippers such as Hoegaarden White to heavy stouts such as Young's Double Chocolate.

Specialty Stores, Markets & Producers

Dynasty Supermarket Barbecue, 9600 Bellaire Blvd., Houston, TX 77036; (713) 995-9832. This great little grocery store offers all kinds of Asian specialties for very reasonable prices. Why is "barbecue" part of the name? Because there's a fantastic little barbecue shack located inside. Order up barbecue pork, roast pork, or even chicken feet. It's definitely worth a try for lunch or dinner.

Then browse the store, paying special attention to the freezer and seafood selections. There's also a wonderful Taiwanese selection here.

Hong Kong Food Market, 11205 Bellaire Blvd., Houston, TX 77036; (281) 575-7886. This store sits as the flagship of Hong Kong City Mall, one of the largest indoor malls in the United States, with more than 20 restaurants and cafes and many shops, gardens, and fountains. The market is part of a national Asian supermarket chain that offers a wide range of products—both grocery and retail. The produce section in particular is incredible, with hard-to-find vegetables and fruits in every color of the rainbow. The frozen selection is also fascinating, with products ranging from soy-based fake meats to desserts to seafood. If you're doing some cooking, missing something from your childhood, or simply feeling adventurous, this is the place to come. Oh, and there are a variety of restaurants inside as well. Other locations are at 5708 S. Gessner Dr. and 13400 Veterans Memorial Dr.

Leibman's Wine & Fine Foods, 14529 Memorial Dr., Houston, TX 77079; (281) 493-3663; www.leibmans.com. Opened in 1979 by Ettienne Leibman and her husband, Ralf, after emigrating from South Africa, Leibman's Wine & Fine Foods has continued to offer a wonderful selection of hard-to-find foods and beverages. Among the offerings: mustards, balsamic vinegars, cooking sauces and rubs, fair-traded coffee, tea, fine chocolates, South African imports, gift baskets, and holiday-related products. There's also a deli with items such as a chicken salad sandwich, turkey and swiss po'boy, grilled eggplant panini, tortilla soup, and more. Catering is also available.

99 Ranch Market, 1005 Blalock Rd., Houston, TX 77055; (713) 932-8899; www.99ranch.com. Established in 1984, this chain of Asian supermarkets offers a variety of products tailored to the needs of the local community. Expect a full-service bakery (and it's really, really good); exotic produce selection (which is typically cheaper than regular grocery stores); a diverse meat and seafood department; wide aisles; and a mix of Japanese, Chinese, Korean, and Vietnamese products. There are even restaurants inside the supermarket where you can find daily specials. Granted, it can get crowded during certain times of the week, but it's worth the trouble to make a visit.

Pete's Fine Meats, 5509 Richmond Ave., Houston, TX 77056; (713) 782-3470; www.petesfinemeats.net. I was happy to stumble upon Pete's Fine Meats, one of the few meat-market and butcher shops I've been able to find in the area. Offering services that range from processing and cooking your wild game to hosting hamburger cookouts for your parents' 50th wedding anniversary, Pete's Fine Meats has your carnivore-centered interests in mind. In the deli expect to find dozens of meats for order, including everything from whole suckling pig and pecan-smoked bacon to free-range chicken and tamales. More exotic meats are also available, such as kangaroo filets, wild boar, turtle, emu kebabs, and ostrich. Closed Sun.

Phoenicia Specialty Foods, 12141 Westheimer Rd., Houston, TX 77077; (281) 558-8225; www.phoeniciafoods.com. With 55,000 square feet of space, you know it's going to take quite a variety of foods to fill this massive warehouse. And quite a variety is exactly what you'll find. Phoenicia Specialty Foods specializes in importing more than 6,000 gourmet items from more than 50 countries around the world. Expect fresh-baked breads, European pastries, hard-to-find wine and beer, fresh seafood, meats and cheeses, prepared foods, exotic produce, chocolate spreads, olives, spices, cookies, tea, and vinegars. Basically, if it's food related and you're looking for it, you can probably find it here. Phoenicia also offers full-service catering. A second location is at 1001 Austin St. downtown.

Food Events

The Grand Wine & Food Affair, 445 Commerce Green Blvd., Sugar Land, TX 77478; (713) 747-9463; www.thegrandwineand foodaffair.com. Held annually in April, this fantastic event features more than 100 wineries and chefs who pull out all the stops to impress the hundreds of participants who attend. Expect events such as winemaker lunches, vintner dinners, wine seminars, a grand tasting, a sip-and-stroll event, and an "around the world" bistro brunch. The event usually lasts 3 or 4 days and is a can't-miss for foodies in Houston. Former special guests have included Ed and Susan Auler, founders of Fall Creek Vineyards; Dr. Richard Becker, founder of Becker Vineyards; Merrill Bonarrigo, cofounder of Messina Hof Vineyards; Greg Bruni of Llano Estacado Winery; Raymond Haak, founder of Haak Vineyards and Winery; and Austin Hope, founder of Austin Hope Winery. There's also a grand auction event that includes art, wines, romantic getaways, collectables, and more; proceeds from the auction support the Grand Wine & Food Affair Scholarship Endowment at the University of Houston's Conrad N. Hilton College of Hotel and Restaurant Management. Sponsors include H-E-B, Marriott Sugar Land Town Square, the City of Sugar Land, Fiji Water, Stella Artois, and *Texas Monthly* magazine.

East Houston:
Pasadena, Pearland,
Clear Lake &
Seabrook

The downtown and Inner Loop area may draw the most attention for its gleaming, food-forward fare, but if you head out east, you're likely to find some of the most understated yet absolutely delicious food you've ever tried. Maybe you're tired of your regular haunts and want to try something new. Maybe you're headed out on a road trip and find yourself with a hankering for a sausage sandwich. No matter the reason, a stop in east Houston won't disappoint. Not sure where to start? Try Pearland, one of the fastest-growing suburbs in the nation. Sure, there are a lot of chains in this area, but if you look hard enough, you're also likely to find a number of truly special local restaurants, such as the wonderfully upscale Killen's Steakhouse and the delightful D Caribbean Curry Spot. Heading to Galveston or the Lyndon B. Johnson Space Center? Stop by Clear Lake for wonderful wine, seafood, or a buffet dinner. You'll also find plenty of rustic markets, interesting events, and fun, food-related shops in this portion of Houston.

Foodie Faves

Barbed Rose Steakhouse and Seafood Co., 113 E. Sealy St., Alvin, TX 77511; (281) 585-2272; www.barbedrose.com; Steak House; $$$. Sure, it's a little bit of a trek from downtown Houston, but it's well worth the effort to get to this young but very well managed steak house and seafood restaurant. Expect a nice range here, from classic steak house and seafood fare such as crab cakes, baked potatoes, and pan-seared diver scallops to Texas-infused and Southern specialties such as stuffed Texas quail crawfish with andouille sausage, crispy alligator bites, chicken and sausage gumbo, and barbecue shrimp and grits. There's also an extensive selection of meats (Angus beef, Strauss veal, Berkshire pork, Texas antelope, Axis venison, Muscovy duck, ostrich) that you can pair with a variety of sauces such as blueberry demi, mint chimichurri, rosemary cream, or miso tartar. Craving a burger? Order one, or head next door to the Burger Bar, where Chef Jason Chaney serves up build-your-own burgers, sandwiches, and seafood plates. For

Executive Chef Jason Chaney's recipe for **Chile-Rubbed Flat Iron Steak with Bacon Tomato Jam,** see p. 200.

see p. 200.

Center Court Pizza and Brew, 9721 Broadway, Ste. 101, Pearland, TX 77584; (713) 436-3927; www.centercourtpizza .com; American; $$. Part pizza shop, part sports bar, Center Court Pizza and Brew impresses with its tangy, homemade sauce and perfectly tossed house-

made dough. The varieties are also impressive, among them: the Ninja Turtle (basic pizza loaded with pepperoni and cheese), the Herbivore (bell peppers, black and green olives, onions, mushrooms, spinach, and tomatoes), Buffalo Chicken (grilled chicken, wing sauce, red onions, and mozzarella with a ranch drizzle); and Sam's Special (grilled chicken, fresh goat cheese, and spinach). Not in the mood for pizza? Try a sandwich, salad, pasta, or dessert. Oh, and the appetizer list here reads like a frat boy's dream: mozzarella cheese dunkers, spinach artichoke dip, fried pickles, pepperoni rolls, bacon cheese fries, spinach egg rolls, and appetizer pizzas. There's also a fully stocked bar with cocktails, beer, and wine. A second location is at 7425 Highway 6, Ste. 100, in Missouri City.

Central Texas Style Barbecue, 4110 W. Broadway, Pearland, TX 77581; (281) 485-9626; www.centralbbq.com; Barbecue; $$. This little joint claims to serve up the best barbecue in Texas, which is a mighty claim in a state where barbecue shacks are about as ubiquitous as McDonald's. But the barbecue here, which is hickory smoked in one of two pits for hours, is quite good. Meat options include sliced beef, chopped beef, sausage links, jalapeño sausage, smoked ham, chicken on the bone, chicken breast, pork loin, turkey breast, pork ribs, and pulled pork. The real standout? Probably the pulled pork, although the sliced beef and pork ribs definitely give it a run for its money. Be sure to try the lunch plate special, which includes 3 or 4 meat options, sides—such as Spanish rice, mustard greens, black beans, green beans, baked beans, and potato salad—and dessert. Sandwiches, a vegetable plate, and extras such as jalapeño corn bread, stuffed jala-peños, deviled eggs, and baked potatoes are also available. For dessert (which you must save room for) go for the banana pudding, the peach cobbler, or the lemon bars. Yum. Open daily from 10 a.m. to 9 p.m.

Chabuca's Restaurant, 316 W. NASA Road 1, Webster, TX 77598; (281) 554-8000; www.chabucas.com; Southern; $$. Craving meat? You've found your place. Whether you want it grilled, fried, broiled, or baked, there's something here you'll want to try. Focused on steaks and rotisserie cooking, Chabuca's serves up an interesting menu. Not sure what you want? Try the American Rotisserie, where $34.95 gets you a choice of 2 salads, 2 vegetables, bread, and all-you-can-eat carvings of more than a dozen meats including spicy six-pepper sirloin, grilled duck a l'orange, fried Louisiana gator

Kemah Boardwalk

Despite being badly battered by 2008's Hurricane Ike, the **Kemah Boardwalk** (215 Kipp Ave. in Kemah; 281-535-8113; www.kemahboardwalk.com) is now back and better than ever. It's a particularly great place to go with the family because of the on-site arcade and amusement park that features a double-decker carousel, a Ferris wheel, a miniature train, a roller coaster, and a speedboat thrill ride. Once you've worked up a sufficient appetite, that's where the real fun begins: There are more than a dozen wonderful places to grab a bite. Among the best:

Bayside Grille, (281) 334-5351. Need a quick breakfast or lunch? Pop into Bayside Grille, where coffee, beignets, croissants, soups, salads, and paninis are the order of the day.

Cadillac Bar, (281) 334-9049; www.cadillacbar.com. This fun restaurant offers all of your favorite Tex-Mex treats, from sizzling fajitas to perfectly mixed margaritas. A great place if you're traveling with a big group.

The Flying Dutchman, (281) 334-7575. Want upscale seafood in a comfortable atmosphere? Look no further than the Flying Dutchman,

tail, grilled leg of lamb, and chicken and apple sausage. You can also get a smaller sample platter that includes many of the same items. There's also a dinner buffet, a large list of dinner steaks, and a Sunday brunch that includes options such as sirloin and cheese which offers seafood, pasta, chicken, Cajun specialties, and steaks overlooking the water.

Lighthouse Buffet, (281) 334-3360. Feeling particularly hungry? Try out this impressive buffet, where 75 feet of food includes soup, salad, entrees, and children's items. The festive nautical themes here are an added bonus.

The Pizza Oven, (281) 334-2228. If you're traveling with kids, this is a great place to consider thanks to its fantastic variety of thin-crust pizzas, salads, and sandwiches. Order up a pizza pie and be ready to stay for a while.

Red Sushi & Hibachi Grill, (281) 334-6708; www.red-sushi.com. Prefer your seafood when it's not exactly cooked? Head over to Red Sushi & Hibachi Grill, which serves up traditional Japanese food and hand-crafted sushi, sashimi, specialty rolls, fish, steaks, tempura, and more. Japanese sake and beer are also available.

Saltgrass Steak House, (281) 538-5441; www.saltgrass.com. Sometimes nothing less than a wonderful steak will do. At those times you need to head to Saltgrass Steak House, a local chain that features certified Angus beef steaks as well as chicken, seafood, and fantastic desserts.

quesadillas, Belgian waffles with strawberries and cream, crispy fried bacon, buttermilk biscuits and cream gravy, and custom eggs and omelets for $9.95. The place may look small and unassuming, but trust me—the food is dependable and affordable.

D Caribbean Curry Spot, 2548 Broadway, Pearland, TX 77581; (281) 412-0849; www.dcaribbeancurryspot.com; Caribbean; $$. This place is a can't-miss for unique, delicious food when in Pearland. The food is exceptional, particularly the dinner plates, which include oxtail, jerk chicken, *pelau* (a meat and brown rice mixture), a Chinese-style chicken dinner, and Bake & Saltfish ("Feel like you are in the Caribbean when you eat this meal," the website assures). There's also a full selection of roti flatbread served with various items including beef, shrimp, vegetables, chicken, duck, and goat. The food is seriously delicious, and authentic. And the friendly owners are happy to let you try something before you order it.

The Egg & I, 557 W. Bay Area Blvd., Webster, TX 77598; (281) 338-8025; www.theeggandirestaurants.com; Breakfast; $$. This chain of breakfast and lunch joints has been expanding rapidly around the country in recent years, and that's a good thing. Known for reliably tasty breakfast fare such as eggs Benedict, omelets, waffles, and pancakes, it's nice to have them located conveniently around the Houston area. The Webster location is a prime example of what this chain is doing

right. Among my favorite dishes: the turkey sausage and eggs (2 fresh eggs cooked to order with 3 turkey sausage patties, ranch potatoes, and toast or English muffins), the Texas skillet (seasoned steak strips, roasted red and green peppers, onions, and portobello mushrooms on ranch potatoes with melted cheese, 2 eggs any style, and an English muffin), and the Flapper (an extra-large whole-wheat pancake, 2 eggs, and 2 strips of bacon or sausage patties). At this reliable, dependable, and affordable place, you won't go wrong. Open weekdays from 6 a.m. to 2 p.m. and weekends from 6 a.m. to 2:30 p.m.

Floyd's Cajun Seafood and Texas Steakhouse, 1300 E. Broadway., Pearland, TX 77581; (281) 993-8385; www.floydssea food.com; Seafood; $$. Talk about two things Texans love: steak and Cajun food. At Floyd's they merge to create the perfect, completely satisfying menu filled with dishes you'll be talking about for weeks. Menu favorites include Floyd's famous seafood salad with lump crabmeat and shrimp; barbecue crab; boiled crawfish; seafood gumbo in dark roux with crabmeat and shrimp; chicken and sausage gumbo; crabmeat-stuffed fried jalapeños; and seafood fondue with lump crabmeat, shrimp, crawfish, and mushrooms in a creamy sauce with garlic toast. And those are just the starters. For entrees, consider anything from frog legs to Bub's Shrimp Platter (6 fried shrimp and 4 shrimp and oyster brochettes with dirty rice and potatoes Floyd) to grilled catfish with red beans and rice. Or try a fresh catch of the day or Texas rib eye steak. There's also a stellar lunch menu with burgers, po'boys, and fried platters served weekdays until 2 p.m. Additional locations are at 20760 Gulf Fwy. in Webster and 2290 I-10 South in Beaumont.

Gilhooley's Restaurant and Oyster Bar, 222 9th St., Dickinson, TX 77539; (281) 339-3813; Seafood; $. Talk about seafood with soul. This affordable restaurant and oyster bar is oozing with character, from its run-down exterior to the, er, colorful artwork on the walls. In this restaurant located near the bay, everything you order tastes fresh, from the just-shucked topped and grilled oysters to the boudin, crab cakes, shrimp cocktail, seafood gumbo, and even burgers. Pets and kids aren't allowed here, however, so if you're looking for a family meal, look elsewhere. But if you're up for a drink and some delicious, cheap seafood, this is the place for you.

Killen's Steakhouse, 2804 S. Main St., Pearland, TX 77581; (281) 485-0844; www.killenssteakhouse.com; Steak House; $$$. Most of Houston's great steak houses may be located inside the Loop, but it's always nice to venture out and try something new. That's why I love Killen's, which proves a restaurant doesn't have to be in downtown Houston to be delicious. Located in the heart of Pearland, Killen's serves Allen Brothers USDA prime beef expertly prepared by Chef Ronnie Killen. Start with an order of jumbo lump crab cake or Nueske bacon–wrapped jumbo scallops, followed by French onion soup or a beefsteak tomato salad. But be sure to save room for one of the main entrees, which include fried chicken with mashed potatoes and *haricots verts;* chicken Francese with mushroom artichoke cream sauce and creamy tomato basil penne pasta; spinach and crab fettuccini pasta tossed with lemon butter, spinach, jumbo lump crab, and sun-dried tomatoes; and a variety of wet- and dry-aged beef. Sides include creamed spinach, sweet potato fries, American steak fries, macaroni and cheese, sautéed mushrooms, and creamed corn. Prices here can be a bit high, but the food is worth the cost.

Little Tokyo, 8201 Broadway, Ste. 101, Pearland, TX 77581; (281) 485-0297; www.littletokyosushi.net; Japanese; $$. Craving sushi? You can't miss a trip to Little Tokyo, where fresh rolls at reasonable prices are the name of the game. Expect a variety of favorite rolls such as the Hana (salmon, avocado, and crab), Cleopatra (salmon, crab, avocado, apple, shrimp tempura, soy paper), Houston (salmon, yellowtail, eel, avocado, green onion, fish eggs, and teriyaki sauce), and the J-eel Hop (freshwater eel, cucumber, avocado, *ikura,* super white tuna, wasabi, fried shrimp, Japanese mayo, and teriyaki sauce). Not in the mood for a roll? Choose from other options ranging from fresh sashimi and hot and sour soup to chicken curry rice and sautéed noodles with beef, chicken, or seafood. A second location is at 6737 Fairmont Pkwy. in Pasadena.

Masa Sushi Japanese Restaurant, 977 Nasa Pkwy., Clear Lake, TX 77598; (281) 486-9888; www.masasushitexas.foodcoral.com; Japanese; $$. Serving up surprisingly good Japanese fusion cuisine, Masa Sushi is a great place to grab a bite for lunch or dinner. At lunch you can get great specials on sushi and sashimi or even grab a bento box with a lunch-size portion of chicken or beef teriyaki, chicken *katsu,* grilled salmon, shrimp tempura, or sautéed vegetables with soup, salad, and rice starting around $7. Going for dinner? There's a wide variety of appetizers and entrees. I recommend any of the rolls or sashimi offerings, as well as the hibachi plates and *udons*. They also have frequent weekly specials, such as ladies' night, when free Champagne is offered, and other drink specials throughout the week. I also love the '80s and '90s music blasting on the radio. A second location is at 1804 FM 646 West in Dickinson.

Mediterraneo Market and Cafe, 18033 Upper Bay Rd., Nassau Bay, TX 77058; (281) 333-3180; www.mediterraneomarket .com; Greek; $$. Part gourmet market, part fantastic little deli, Mediterraneo Market impresses with both its selection and the quality of its food. Open for lunch and dinner, it offers menu options including sandwiches and pita wraps, soups, salads, vegetarian plates (falafel, dolmas, hummus, baba ghanoush, and taboulleh with pita bread—yum!), and Mediterraneo plates such as a gyros plate, lamb kebab plate, grilled chicken plate, and baked kibbe plate (beef and pine nuts served with baba ghanoush). Lasagna and spaghetti are also available. And don't miss the delicious desserts, including a dark chocolate tart with flourless almond crust, crème brûlée, baklava, and fantastic tiramisu. Open daily except Sun.

O'Cajcen Seafood Restaurant, 1635 Broadway, Ste. 117, Pearland, TX 77581; (281) 993-1779; www.ocajcenseafood.com; Seafood; $$. As you can probably guess by the name of this joint, the reason to come to O'Cajcen Seafood Restaurant is the seafood. Expect seafood in all varieties—po'boys, crawfish, gumbo, étouffée, fried platters, shrimp, lobster, and steak. The original owners were from New Orleans and managed to infuse the place with those cooking traditions. Open daily except Sun.

Peppers Beef & Seafood, 3604 Fairmont Pkwy., Pasadena, TX 77504; (281) 998-1114; http://peppersrestaurant.net; Southern; $$. Peppers calls itself "the best-kept secret in the South," and it's certainly one of the lesser-known restaurants in the Houston area. But don't let that stop you from trying it out. The fare here, which revolves around steak and seafood, is top-notch. Start with an order of the delicious seafood-stuffed fried mushrooms or stuffed jalapeños. In the mood for pasta? Don't miss the seafood primavera (think Gulf shrimp, crabmeat, crawfish tails, and veggies tossed with Alfredo sauce and fettuccini) or the crawfish pasta Monica, which comes with crawfish tails sautéed in a Cajun cream sauce over fettuccini pasta. The real reason to come here, however, is the steaks, from the top sirloin to the Texas T-bone to the chopped sirloin steak, which is 10 ounces of charbroiled ground beef with sautéed onions, mushrooms, and brown gravy. The peppercorn rib eye tenderloin medallions are another standout. Cuts are seasoned with fresh herbs and slow roasted with au jus and whipped horseradish sauce. It may be in the middle of nowhere, but with its affordable prices and dependable food, Peppers is worth a visit.

Seabrook Classic Cafe, 2511 Nasa Pkwy., Seabrook, TX 77586; (281) 326-1512; www.seabrookclassiccafe.com; Southern; $$. This is a good old classic cafe, plain and simple, and you can't miss with a trip here for lunch or dinner. In addition to staples such as chicken-fried steak, prime rib and seafood combos, liver and onions, and fettuccini Alfredo, the cafe has also taken great pains to update its menu with items for "the next 25 years." These include Midwest meat loaf (ground pork and beef with whipped potatoes, brown Shiner Bock gravy, fresh green beans with bacon and red onion, and focaccia), Southern fried chicken (fried chicken breast and leg with whipped potatoes, cream gravy, green beans, and focaccia), and the Cuban sandwich (ham, pork, swiss cheese, pickles, and mustard, grilled and pressed, served with steak fries and dipping sauce from the Caribbean). Don't miss the incredible Benson Burger (½-pound burger with mayo, jalapeños, horseradish, cheese, and Worcestershire).

Sudie's Seafood House, 352 N. Gulf Fwy., League City, TX 77373; (281) 338-5100; www.sudies.com; Seafood; $$. This family-owned restaurant has been well-known in the Houston area since 1983 thanks to its delicious fare from the sea. Whether you order up fried catfish or something fresh from the fish-of-the-day board, or go an entirely different direction with chicken-fried steak or a 12-ounce rib eye, you'll leave here satisfied. Among the favorite menu items: seafood fondue with blackened shrimp and crawfish as well as mushrooms, spinach, creamy Magnolia

sauce, and Monterey Jack cheese served with garlic toast; loaded baked potato soup; the Blackened Tupelo (2 fillets of blackened catfish with sautéed shrimp and crawfish in a lemon garlic butter sauce with rice pilaf and mixed vegetables); and a seafood platter with 2 catfish fillets, 4 oysters, 4 scallops, 4 fried shrimp, 4 boiled shrimp, and a stuffed crab. Great drink specials are also available. A second location is at 4910 Spencer Hwy. in Pasadena.

Specialty Stores, Markets & Producers

Lyndon B. Johnson Space Center, 2101 Nasa Pkwy., Houston, TX 77586; (281) 483-0123; www.spacecenter.org. I know this may seem like an odd listing under "specialty stores, markets & producers," but hear me out. If you live in or visit Houston, chances are good that at some point you'll end up at the Johnson Space Center to spend a day contemplating all things air and space. While you're there, it's worth a gander at the gift shop, where some specialty food items just might strike your fancy. Ever had astronaut ice cream? You can get it here. Want to sample "space food sticks"? You're covered. Don't want to make the trip out to the Space Center? You can also order many of these products online.

Oaxaca Meat Market, 4339 FM 517 East, Dickinson, TX 77539; (281) 534-8790. This is a hole-in-the-wall in the middle of nowhere, and perhaps that's what makes it so great. At the Oaxaca Meat Market, you can find a variety of fantastic products—namely meat—from the Oaxaca area of Mexico. If you're cooking, head directly to the meat counter, where you'll find things you can't even name. If you're hungry, the deli is ready with products ranging from hamburgers to tamales to flautas. You can also grab a bag of homemade pork rinds to go.

Food Events

Blessing of the Fleet Gumbo Cookoff and Parade, each spring in Kemah; (281) 334-3181; www.kemah.net/blessing.html. This beloved event is fun for boat owners and spectators alike thanks to the variety of events it includes. If you own a boat, you can enter it in the boat parade and have it blessed by a Catholic priest and Protestant minister for the upcoming summer season. Then participate in the parade, which is followed by an awards ceremony where prizes and trophies are given for the best decorated boats. A shrimp gumbo cook-off is also part of the weekend of festivities.

Clear Lake Area Chamber of Commerce Epicurian Evening, Space Center Houston, 1601 NASA Pkwy., Houston, TX 77058; (281) 488-7676; www.clearlakearea.com/events/epicureanevening.asp. This annual event includes an evening of food samples, live entertainment, shopping, a silent auction, and a kids' area sponsored by more than 40 area restaurants and establishments. Former participants have included **Cadillac Bar** (see p. 148), **D'Vine Wine of Kemah and Galveston, Edible Arrangements, Floyd's Cajun Seafood and Texas Steakhouse** (see p. 151), **Flying Dutchman** (see p. 148), **Freebirds World Burritos, Galveston College and Culinary Arts Academy, Mamacita's Mexican Restaurant and Cantina, Red River BBQ & Grill, Red Sushi & Hibachi Grill** (see p. 149), **Crazy Alan's Swamp Shack,** and **Tradicao Brazilian Steakhouse.** Adult tickets are $30 in advance, $35 at the door; tickets are $10 for children ages 4 to 12 and free for children 3 and under.

Pasadena Taste of the Town, Pasadena Convention Center, 7902 Fairmont Pkwy., Pasadena, TX 77507; www.pasadenachamber .org/taste.html. Hosted by the Pasadena Chamber of Commerce, the Pasadena Taste of the Town is usually held in the fall and regularly draws more than 3,000 people eager to try the best from more than 30 area restaurants. Expect food booths representing American, seafood, and ethnic cuisines as well as dessert and beverage stations. Adult tickets are $25 in advance, $30 at the door. Children's tickets are $15 for ages 6–12 and free for children 5 and under. Tickets are available online for purchase.

Allegria Wine Bar and Cocktail Lounge, 15210 Highway 3, Webster, TX 77598; (281) 218-8585; www.allegriawinebar.com. It may be located in a strip mall, but Allegria Wine Bar and Cocktail Lounge is definitely worth a trip. What you'll find after you walk in the door is a full bar that emphasizes great wines—more than 40 of them, as a matter of fact. You can order wine by the glass, half bottle, or bottle, as well as aperitifs, beer, scotch, martinis, coffee, tea, and premium liquor. Hungry? Try out something from a limited menu that includes petite crab cakes, personal flatbread pizzas, spinach and artichoke puff pastry, and hot and cold hors d'oeuvres. Added bonus: It's pet friendly and frequently features live music.

Big Texas Dance Hall and Saloon, 803 E. NASA Road 1, Webster, TX 77598; (281) 461-4400; www.bigtexassaloon.com. If you've ever wanted to hit up an authentic Texas dance hall with an impressive drink selection, Big Texas Dance Hall and Saloon is the place for you. And it's cheap, too. Regular drink specials include $1.25 domestic longnecks, wells, call drinks, and house wine on Wednesdays; happy hour from 6 to 9 p.m. and $1.75 select domestic longnecks all night on Thursday; $1.75 domestic beer, wells, calls, and house wine and $2.75 Crown Royal drinks all night on Friday; and happy hour from 7 to 10 p.m. and no cover until 9 p.m. on Saturday. The live music here is really great, too, featuring wonderful touring acts such as the Randy Rogers Band, the Scooter Brown Band, and the Cody Johnson Band. A second location is at 19959 Holzwarth Rd. in Spring.

Boondoggles Pub and Pizzeria, 4106 NASA Pkwy., Ste. D, El Lago, 77586; (281) 326-2739; www.boondogglespub.com. Boondoggles Pub and Pizzeria has long been a local favorite for its fantastic food and drink selection, but it's quickly gaining a reputation outside of the Clear Lake area as well. When you come here, you can expect a full menu. Appetizers alone range from seviche to soft pretzels to pizza chips (pizza crust topped with provolone and Parmesan cheese and oregano). As you can probably guess from the name, one of the main draws here is the pizza, which is served on a thin crust with various toppings. My favorite is the Jambalaya pizza, with crawfish, shrimp, andouille sausage, Romano, provolone cheese, and Creole sauce. Sandwiches, burgers, salads, and chicken dishes are also available. And let's not forget the bar offerings. There are dozens of beers on tap here, ranging from Boddington's Pub Ale to Stella Artois to Real Ale Rio Blanco Pale Ale. Daily specials include Monday steak night, snow crab and shrimp on Thursday, bloody Marys and mimosas on Saturday, and Sunday brunch from 11 a.m. to 2 p.m.

Chelsea Wine Bar, 4106 NASA Pkwy., Seabrook, TX 77586; (281) 326-5282; www.chelseawinebartexas.com. This place is cool, calm, collected, and cheap—a wonderful place to waste away a Sunday afternoon. Expect a variety of live music here as well as low-priced wines and frequent food specials. The intimate, dimly lit ambience makes it great for a date night, although it's also a comfortable place to catch up with friends or even sit by yourself and read a book. The coffee and beer selection here is also excellent, as are the views, which overlook the lake. There's a $10 rib eye special on Sunday, and don't miss the delightful cheese board.

Haak Vineyards & Winery, 6310 Avenue T, Santa Fe, TX 77510; (409) 925-1401; www.haakwine.com. Located about 40 minutes from downtown Houston, this little vineyard and winery is a wonderful place to spend an afternoon. Here, Raymond and Gladys Haak have been turning out delicious, local wines on 3 acres with 1,800 vines since 2000. First wander the vineyard, then take a tour of the 25,000-square-foot winery, where an 1,800-square-foot cellar holds wine-filled oak barrels. Tours are offered daily on the hour for $5 a person and include 4 tastings of Haak wines, such as the 2010 Estate Reserve Blanc du Bois, 2009 Cabernet Sauvignon, and the Pink Pelican NV. The winery is open Mon through Fri from 11 a.m. to 6 p.m., Sat from 11 a.m. to 7 p.m., and Sunday from noon to 5 p.m. Special events, including wonderful summer weekend concerts, are held frequently. Check the website for details.

Three Oaks Fine Wines and Exquisite Foods, 601 E. Main St., League City, TX 77573; (281) 557-8466; www.3oaks.net. This fun, intimate wine dive is a great place to go for a date or to meet up with friends. Expect great happy hour specials and a wide selection of wines. The menu here is also impressive. Special events include ladies' night with chocolate-dipped strawberries for female customers, wine and dinner pairings, and live jazz.

On the Outskirts: Galveston, Brenham & Bryan

Okay, so you want to get away for a weekend. You're tired of the hustle and bustle of the city, the traffic along the major highways, and the same old restaurants and shops that you visit day after day. Then it's time, my friend, for you to take a road trip. And since you're in Houston, you're in luck, because there are a number of wonderful places for foodies to visit.

My first recommendation, of course, is Galveston. A simple one-hour drive will automatically transport you to a tight-knit beach community with some of the most wonderful seafood you've ever had. Not a seafood fan? Never fear. There are plenty of other restaurant types as well, from incredible homemade pizza at Mario's Ristorante to perfect petits fours at PattyCakes Bakery. In the mood to do some shopping? You're in luck as well. Because Galveston is a major hub for cruise lines, most shops are open year-round and offer a full selection of goodies. Stop in at Old Strand Emporium for some "bathtub wine," or drop in at La King's Confectionary for a hand-dipped shake or fresh pulled taffy.

Already done Galveston? Some other places to consider include Bryan, home to Messina Hof, one of the greatest vineyards and wineries in the state, and Brenham, which in addition to being home to the incredible Blue Bell Creamery is filled with country-style fare you'll absolutely enjoy.

Foodie Faves

Benno's on the Beach, 1200 Seawall Blvd., Galveston, TX 77550; (409) 762-4621; www.bennosofgalveston.com; Seafood; $$. If you ask Galveston natives about the best seafood in the city, a good number of them will probably say Benno's on the Beach, which has been serving up quality seafood since 1983. The atmosphere here is totally casual (think checkered tablecloths and counter service). And because the specialty is Cajun-inspired seafood, the dishes you'll find here are different—and frequently more interesting—than more upscale restaurants in town. Menu items include crawfish tails, whole catfish (weighing in at a full pound), Cajun-seasoned chicken, blackened oysters, crawfish étouffée, shrimp gumbo, red beans and rice, jambalaya, hush puppies, and Cajun potatoes. And don't miss the bread pudding with bourbon sauce or key lime pie for dessert. Tip: If you want something really remarkable and fresh, order from the "below the menu" menu, which lists special items currently in season.

Bernardo's Restaurant at the Hotel Galvez, 2024 Seawall Blvd., Galveston, TX 77550; (409) 765-7721; www.wyndham.com; Southern; $$. The view from this airy restaurant with huge windows in the heart of the Hotel Galvez is stunning, as is the fare, which centers on fresh Gulf Coast seafood. The ideal time to try out Bernardo's is during its famous Sunday brunch, which is offered from 11 a.m. to 2 p.m. and features dishes such as Belgian waffles, pastries, a prime rib carving station, a pasta station, an omelet station, soups, salads, pastries, eggs Benedict, desserts, bottomless Champagne and mimosas, and hot entrees that change weekly. The cost is $32 for adults. Reservations are recommended.

Cajun Greek, 2226 61st St., Galveston, TX 77551; (409) 744-7041; www.galveston.com/cajungreek; Cajun; $$. Okay, so the name is a little weird, but don't let that keep you from trying this island gem. Featuring fresh seafood and Cajun-inspired specialties, Cajun Greek is a must-try when you're in Galveston. The Greek salad is a standout (as it should be, based on the restaurant name), as are other Greek dishes that grace the menu. And if you're craving a hamburger, be sure to order one—this is a haven for beef lovers. Save room for chocolate pecan cake for dessert. Open daily for lunch and dinner except Tues.

Casey's Seafood Cafe, 3800 Seawall Blvd., Galveston, TX 77550; (409) 762-9625; www.gaidos.com; Seafood; $$. A more affordable alternative to upscale big brother Gaido's, Casey's Seafood Cafe still manages to serve some of the best seafood on the island. I recommend grabbing a table on the sprawling outside patio, which offers wonderful views of the ocean and nice, cool breezes. Menu items here include deep-fried zucchini, a bay shrimp and avocado BLT, lobster tacos, the famous Juicy Lucy (a bacon burger covered with chili *con queso*), Southwest garlic fried chicken, seafood platters, and the bay shrimp salad, which is one of the best salads I've ever eaten. A full selection of cocktails, wines, and draft and bottled beer are also available. I recommend the Raspberry Sea Breeze, which includes fresh-squeezed Ruby Red grapefruit juice mixed with cranberry juice, ripe raspberries, and Smirnoff vodka. Finish up your meal with one of many dessert offerings, such as Seven Layers of Heaven chocolate cake, Paulie Gaido's Crustless Pecan Pie, and Casey's vanilla soft-serve.

Dibella's Italian Restaurant, 1902 31st St., Galveston, TX 77550; (409) 763-9036; www.galveston.com/dibellas; Italian; $$. Looking for authentic Italian? You've come to the right place. Dibella's is a local favorite for its incredible variety of Italian fare, ranging from veal piccata to made-to-order rib eye. If you go, be prepared to leave stuffed—all entrees and specialties come with antipasto garlic bread, soup or salad, and choice of pasta. Among the best dishes here: shrimp scampi, lasagna, tortellini, ravioli, and french-bread pizza. It's not particularly cheap—most dishes will run you $15 to $20—but most of the entrees are well worth it, particularly given the amount of food you get. Lunch and dinner are served daily except Mon.

Dylan's Bar and Grill, 8601 9th Ave., Port Arthur, TX 77642; (409) 722-1600; www.dylanson9th.com; American; $$. This place has no windows, which kind of makes it look like it may have once been a strip club, but these days it's a family-friendly joint serving up some delicious pub grub. Among the items we tried: fried oyster shooters, hush puppies, kitchen-sink *queso,* and potato skins. There's also a full line of soups; salads (including Caesar, Cobb, chef, grilled tuna, and chicken tender); and sandwiches such as the black and blue buffalo sandwich, a Monterey mushroom chicken sandwich, a fried chicken wrap, and a french dip. And don't forget to add one of the sides, which include steamed veggies, Cajun fries, coleslaw, mashed potatoes, green beans, guacamole, and house-battered onion rings. Daily specials include prime rib and live music on Tuesday, happy hour until 11 p.m. on Monday and Wednesday, $1 off all burgers and bottle beers on Thursday, and live music and buckets of beer on special on Friday.

Eatcetera, 408 25th St., Galveston, TX 77550; (409) 762-0803; www.eatcetera.net; European; $$. You don't hear about Eatcetera as much as you hear about some of the other restaurants in Galveston, but trust me when I tell you this little joint holds its own. The vibe here is unique gourmet, with fresh, local ingredients and menu items that may otherwise be difficult to find on the island. By that, I mean options such as a Thai beef sandwich with carrots and daikon radish; a grilled asparagus and roasted onion sandwich with blue cheese cream; a fontina cheese, sun-dried tomato, and bell pepper panini; smoked Norwegian salmon salad; hominy and new potato soup; and desserts that include spumoni cheesecake, Tortuga rum cake, and forest berry tart with organic vanilla ice cream. Daily specials are also available. Closed Sun.

Farmhouse Cafe, 1004 14th St., Huntsville, TX 77340; (936) 435-1450; www.farmhousecafe.net; Southern; $$. This local Huntsville institution regularly sports a parking lot filled with cars, and that's a good thing. When you come here, expect fresh, down-home food and a super friendly staff ready to fill your table (and tummy) with items such as coconut shrimp, baby spinach, and fresh strawberry salad (served with homemade strawberry dressing—yum), a double-decker BLT, and chicken-fried steak and chicken. Signature dishes include the blue-plate special, which changes daily and comes with 2 sides, as well as pepper fried steak and the classic club. And don't miss the fried green tomatoes when they're in season.

Fisherman's Wharf, 2200 Harborside Dr., Galveston, TX 77550; (409) 765-5708; www.fishermanswharfgalveston.com; Seafood; $$$. This restaurant is owned by Landry's, and if there's one thing the Landry's corporation knows, it's seafood. Located directly on the water with a magnificent view of the tall ship *Elissa,* Fisherman's Wharf is a great place for casual (if not slightly overpriced) seafood in a comfortable, clean atmosphere. Grab a seat outside and start with a helping of crab *queso* (that's crabmeat, spinach, and artichoke hearts folded into a rich cheese sauce, served with tortilla chips—it's fantastic) or Shrimp Kisses (Gulf shrimp stuffed with jalapeño Jack cheese, wrapped in bacon, and fried). Follow that up with a cup of crab and lobster bisque or spinach salad. For your entree, consider a crab cake sandwich, lobster and crawfish pasta, a fried oyster dinner, or the Chicken Elissa (10 ounces of char-grilled chicken breast topped with sautéed artichoke hearts, tomatoes, capers, green onions, and mushrooms in a white wine butter sauce served with sautéed new potatoes). Drink and happy hour menus are also available.

Gaido's Seafood Restaurant, 3828 Seawall Blvd., Galveston, TX 77550; (409) 762-9625; www.gaidos.com; Seafood; $$$. **Among** the top tier of the many seafood restaurants in Galveston, Gaido's Seafood Restaurant is an upscale but warm place to get your seafood fix. Founded in 1911 and located along the Galveston Seawall, the restaurant offers delicious fresh seafood and wonderful views of the ocean where it came from. Standout menu items include the Jazz Martini (seasonal seafood tossed with avocados and hearts of palm in a creamy chipotle sauce), a goat cheese salad (pistachio-crusted goat cheese over fresh spinach tossed in raspberry vinaigrette), fried and combination seafood platters, seasonal dishes such as deep sea scallops, and meats such as the 14-ounce Saporito pork chop with crushed crackers and garlic. Or order the Captain's Plate, which comes with a half entree, side, and dessert for the same price as a full entree. Reservations are recommended.

Judge Roy Bean's Coffee Saloon, 5316 Broadway, Ste. A, Galveston, TX 77551; (409) 539-5197; www.jrbcoffee.com; Breakfast; $$. Even though the wonderful little cafe is open for breakfast, lunch, and dinner, the real reason to come here is for a fantastic cup of coffee. Opened in January 2011, Judge Roy Bean's is committed to ordering and serving coffee that will soothe your soul while awakening your mind. Menu offerings include a chicken salad croissant, Louisiana Meat Hand Pie, Louisiana Mud Bug Hand Pie, Frito pie, chicken potpie, and a variety of pastries and breakfast items that include oatmeal, biscuits and gravy, waffles, pastries, cupcakes, pies, cookies, and more. It's dog friendly, too, so Fido is welcome. Open daily.

M&M Restaurant and Bar, 2401 Church St., Galveston, TX 77550; (409) 766-7170; www.mmgalveston.com; Steak House; $$$. Built in 1884, the building where M&M is located stands as a testament to perseverance in Galveston: It survived the 1900 storm and all the hurricanes that have followed. The restaurant itself has also withstood the test of time, with an upscale steak house vibe and a vibrant menu that draw customers in year after year. In terms of cuisine, expect everything from steaks and cheeseburgers to meat and cheese boards and buttermilk fried asparagus. A wonderful Sunday brunch that includes fare such as stuffed french toast, chorizo and eggs, a fried egg sandwich, and a grilled tuna BLT is also offered. Closed Mon.

Mario's Italian Ristorante, 2201 61st St., Galveston, TX 77551; (409) 744-2975; www.mariosristorante.com; Italian; $$. The motto here is, "We speak very little English, but we make the best pizza," and I have to say that's probably true. The bacon and cheese variety I tried was near perfection. Other fun pizza varieties include the Good Health Special (grilled chicken breast with sautéed spinach and mozzarella cheese on whole-wheat crust), the Carnivore (pepperoni, bacon, Italian sausage, and hamburger), and the Vampire Slayer (fresh garlic, green onions, and garlic-infused chicken breast). Start with the garlic cheese bread or an order of fried calamari, followed by a bowl of steaming minestrone or house salad. Not in the mood for pizza? Other menu items include pasta (I like "the twins"—1 ricotta cheese–stuffed pasta roll and 1 meat and spinach–stuffed pasta roll topped with tomato sauce and melted mozzarella), sandwiches, and a variety of seafood and chicken specialties. Be warned, the portions here are huge (I swear my soup order came in a bucket, not a bowl), so you'll want to get a to-go container. A second, more upscale location is at 628 Seawall Blvd.

Mosquito Cafe, 628 14th St., Galveston, TX 77550; (409) 763-1010; www.mosquitocafe.com; Breakfast; $$. Mosquito Cafe serves up so many breakfast offerings on weekends that it will be difficult for you to order only one. Options include a breakfast bowl stuffed with potatoes, fresh spinach, bacon, cheese, and poached eggs; crustless quiche with Italian sausage, swiss cheese, apples, sweet peppers, potatoes, and caramelized onion served with potatoes or fruit; tacos with homemade corned beef hash with potatoes, caramelized onions, and bell peppers stuffed in 3 corn tortillas and served with a side of medium-spicy red sauce and 3 eggs any style. Missed breakfast? Try lunch, when items such as a Southwest green chile burger, Thai chicken salad, spinach pasta, curried ahi tuna salad, and barbecue pork sandwich are sure to strike your fancy. The restaurant is open Tues through Fri for lunch and dinner, Sat for breakfast, lunch, and dinner, and Sun for breakfast all day and lunch. The restaurant is closed Mon.

Must Be Heaven Sandwich Shop, 107 W. Alamo St., Brenham, TX 77833; (979) 830-8536; www.mustbeheaven.com; American; $$. This is the quintessential small-town sandwich shop, with menu items that will satisfy your soul and your stomach. Stop in around lunchtime and be ready to feast on sandwiches such as a french dip

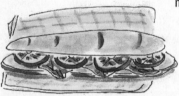

(served hot on toasted french bread), a muffaletta (served hot with homemade marinated green olive dressing), a turkey and swiss club (that includes 5 strips of bacon), and The Works (sliced honey cured ham, mesquite-smoked turkey breast, roast beef, Genoa salami, crispy bacon, and swiss cheese, served hot). All are served with chips, a pickle spear, and a mint. No matter what you order, though, be sure to save room for the desserts, which are the real draw here. The incredible pie selection includes banana coconut pecan pie, coconut cream pie, and, my favorite, apple pie, topped with a big scoop of Blue Bell ice cream. Other locations are at 1136 E. Villa Maria in Bryan, 100 S. Main St. in Bryan, and 1700 Rock Prairie Rd. in College Station.

Olympia Grill, 4908 Seawall Blvd., Galveston, TX 77551; (409) 766-1222; www.olympiagrill.net; Greek; $$. In the mood to get your Greek on? This authentic Greek restaurant might seem out of place in a sand and seafood town such as Galveston, but it's actually a perfect fit for anyone looking for a healthy, flavorful meal. Run by first-generation Greek Americans who were born and raised in Galveston, Olympia Grill offers the perfect mix of Greek cuisine with Galveston sensibilities. When you arrive, start with the Zeus Sampler, which offers a mix of Greek specialties such as hummus, feta cheese, kalamata olives, dolmas, garlic dip, eggplant dip, and yogurt dip, all served with pita bread. Then move on to your main entree, which may include a grilled shrimp pita with lettuce, tomato, and *tzatziki* sauce, a gyro platter served with *tzatziki,* onion, tomato, and pita bread, roasted lamb shank, or beef tenderloin kebabs. Open daily for lunch and dinner. A second location is at Pier 21 and Harborside Drive.

Rudy & Paco Restaurant and Bar, 2028 Post Office St., Galveston, TX 77553; (409) 762-3639; www.rudyandpaco.com; Steak House; $$$. Rudy & Paco calls itself Galveston's most unique dining experience, and after a visit there you're likely to say that's true. It's like a throwback to a 1950s steak house with a little South and Central American flavor thrown in for good measure. The restaurant is conveniently located next to the historic Grand 1894 Opera House, so it's a wonderful place to start out a date night, followed by a show. And be sure to dress to impress—shorts are not allowed in the main dining room at dinner (they are allowed in the bar, however). Menu items here range from escargot to empanadas (1 shrimp, 1 beef, 1 chicken, served with cilantro cream sauce) to fresh Gulf red snapper served with Creole sauce to a 14-ounce New York strip steak. Oh, and don't miss the bread pudding for dessert. The service is top-notch; reservations are recommended. The restaurant is closed Sun.

Shrimp and Stuff, 3901 Avenue O, Galveston, TX 77550; (409) 763-2805; www.shrimpnstuff.com; Seafood; $$. It may not be upscale, but this little restaurant is turning out some of the greatest seafood in Galveston, from seafood dinners to po'boys to gumbos and salads. Open for 30 years, it's become a go-to spot for islanders and visitors alike, who love the pet-friendly patio and the low prices. The entire menu is worth a try, but standout items revolve, not surprisingly, around shrimp dishes such as the fried shrimp basket, the shrimp po'boy, coconut shrimp, and shrimp gumbo. The hush puppies, crab balls, fried oyster, and fish tacos are also well worth a try. Open daily for lunch and dinner.

The Steakhouse at the San Luis Resort, 5222 Seawall Blvd., Galveston, TX 77551; (800) 445-0090; www.sanluisresort.com; Steak House; $$$. Named one of the best restaurants in the state by *Texas Monthly* magazine and the *Galveston County Daily News,* The Steakhouse at the San Luis Resort is a dimly lit, elegant, upscale restaurant that features fresh steak and seafood and a diverse wine list. Menu standouts include escargot; Asian pear salad; sautéed Gulf snapper with premium lump crab; and the steak house cordial dinner for two, which includes beef tenderloin and grilled shrimp with mashed potatoes and asparagus and dessert for $95. Reservations are recommended on weekends. Can't get one? Grab a seat at the swanky bar, where the full menu is available, as well as a bar menu with appetizer selections such as teriyaki chicken, calamari, and sushi. Cutoffs, swimwear, and jean shorts are not permitted; dress shorts and sandals are okay. Closed Sun. Searching for a great cocktail? Head to the poolside H20 Ultra-Lounge for a stiff drink. For H20 Ultra-Lounge's recipe for **Sailor J's Spiced Eggnog,** see p. 206.

Sunflower Bakery and Cafe, 512 14th St., Galveston, TX 77550; (409) 763-5500; www.thesunflowerbakeryandcafe.com; Bakery; $$. Sunflower Bakery and Cafe serves up breakfast, lunch, and dinner, with specialties that range from seafood sandwiches to rich pastries to pastas and salads. My favorite time to come is during breakfast, which includes a bacon and egg sandwich, bread pudding french toast, a shrimp omelet, and filet mignon and eggs. All seafood comes fresh off the dock daily. Got seafood overload? Never fear. Other lunch and dinner options here include chicken-fried steak, steak and fettuccine, a buffalo burger, a deluxe grilled cheese, and a grilled Reuben. Don't miss the wonderful baked goods, either, which include coffee cakes, bundt cakes, cinnamon rolls, tarts, and more. Hours vary by day; check website for details.

Yaga's Cafe, 2314 Strand St., Galveston, TX 77550; (409) 762-6676; www.yagaspresents.com/yagascafe/index.html; Southern; $$. Yaga's Cafe is most certainly a favorite on the island, with fabulous, laid-back lunch and dinner options that make you want to hang out for a while. The menu is filled with beach-inspired classics such as seafood flautas; beef and black bean empanadas; roasted jerk chicken (this is a must-try); coconut shrimp; pizzas (I like the Surfer's Paradise, with ham, pineapple, and mozzarella); and a bunch of burgers that include sliders, the Death Burger (½-pounder with bacon, cheese, mushrooms, jalapeños, and chili), and a veggie burger made with eggplant and served over Spanish rice. In addition, the cafe also offers a variety of weekly specials, such as 12-inch pizzas for $5 and $1 draft beer after 8 p.m. on Thursday, and chicken-fried steak with mashed potatoes and veggies for $8.95 between 6 and 9 p.m. on Wednesday.

Landmarks

Royer's Round Top Cafe, 105 Main St., Round Top, TX 78954; (979) 249-3611; www.royersroundtopcafe.com; American; $$. Royer's is famous for its pies, so it's only fitting that I mention them first. Varieties include Ann's pecan pie, JB's white chocolate chip macadamia nut pie, Bud's chocolate chip pie, Bud's butterscotch chip pie, Cafe's buttermilk pie, Sam's coconut chess pie, D'Ette's strawberry rhubarb pie, sugar-free peach pie, Not-My-Mom's apple pie, and Bob Pastorio's cherry pie. All pies are served with Amy's ice cream. My mouth is watering right now just thinking about them. However, if you can manage to wait to order your pie until after you have a bite to eat, you'll be pleasantly surprised by the lunch and dinner fare as well. The menu includes small-town classics such as a grilled shrimp BLT, a beef tenderloin sandwich, Cafe's smoked bacon salad sandwich, jalapeño cheese soup, and chicken corn chowder with fresh cilantro. There's also a special Sunday fried chicken dinner. The restaurant is open Thurs through Sun.

Specialty Stores, Markets & Producers

Blue Bell Creamery, 1101 S. Blue Bell Rd.; Brenham, TX 77833; (979) 836-7977; www.bluebell.com. The motto here is, "We eat all we can and we sell the rest," and during a tour of the sprawling ice cream factory, you'll find that to ring true. From the employee break room to the expansive gift shop, ice cream is everywhere. And that's a good thing. After all, there's a reason that Brenham-based Blue Bell Ice Cream, which opened in 1907, is among the top three best-selling ice creams in the country. As you watch flavors such as banana pudding, chocolate mud pie, and buttered pecan flow into the cartons on an assembly line and learn fun facts about the company (did you know, for example, that homemade vanilla remains the company's best seller?), you'll be very glad you made the 90-minute trek. Tours are offered Mon through Fri at 10 a.m., 11 a.m., 1 p.m., 1:30 p.m., 2 p.m., and 2:30 p.m.; no tours are offered on weekends. Cost is $5 for adults and $3 for children 6–14 and seniors 55 and over and includes a serving of ice cream.

Burton Sausage Company, 11700 Hwy. 290 West, Brenham, TX 77833; (979) 289-3421; www.burtonsausage.com. Calling itself a "country brand made in a small town with a big taste," Burton Sausage Company doesn't disappoint in terms of flavor, price, or selection. Next time you drive to Austin, bring along a cooler and stop in Brenham at Burton's for some of the freshest sausage, steaks, and jerky you've ever had. How do you know it's fresh? The Burton Sausage Company doubles as a slaughterhouse. Prices are extremely affordable and the sausage is always high quality. Find Burton Sausage, which comes in varieties such as beef, pork, and turkey, at area stores including Albertson's, Brookshire Brothers, Food Town, H-E-B, Kroger, Sellers Brothers, and Walmart.

Chappell Hill Bakery and Deli, 8900 Hwy. 290 East, Chappell Hill, TX 77426; (979) 836-2560. For years, people passing through Chappell Hill on their way to Austin knew to stop at the Chappell Hill Exxon for some of the best kolaches and pastries in the state. Now, thanks to the word of mouth that turned that little gas station into a local culinary legend, the Chappell Hill Bakery and Deli has expanded to take up its own rather large building next door. The benefit for you and me? Even more kolaches, as well as other food items such as barbecue, burgers, and Blue Bell ice cream. Could it get any more fabulously Texan? There is also an assortment of other baked goods, including apple pie, cookies, and blueberry cinnamon rolls.

Chappell Hill Sausage Company, 4255 Sausage Ln., Chappell Hill, TX 77426; (979) 836-5830. I'll gladly visit any place located on Sausage Lane, and this place more than lived up to my expectations. Located right off US 290 about an hour from Houston, the Chappell Hill Sausage Company was established in 1968 with a mission of creating the area's best sausage. Today the company is churning out multiple varieties that include original smoked, smoked garlic, fresh, jalapeño and cheese, smoked green onion, and smoked pork and venison. Other specialty products such as spiral honey-glazed ham, bacon, gift baskets, seasonings, and summer sausage are also available. There's also an on-site restaurant serving sausage, barbecue, and breakfast items. It's open daily except Sun. Can't make it out to Chappell Hill? The company's products are available around Houston at stores such as Kroger, Randalls, Rice Epicurean, Fiesta, H-E-B, and others. Or you can simply order online.

Eckermann's Meat Market, 2543 FM 1457, New Ulm, TX 78950; (979) 836-8858; www.eckermannsmeatmarket.com. Eckermann's Meat Market was founded in 1961 and now turns out a variety of sausage types that include beef-pork with garlic, pure beef sausage, jalapeño smoked sausage, peppered summer sausage, smoked dry sausage with garlic, hot links, and more in its 10,000-square-foot facility. Order online or visit the website to find a list of dozens of stores that sell the sausage in the Houston area. Special orders, gift baskets, and deer processing are also available.

Kountry Boy Sausage, 1909 Longwood Dr., Brenham, TX 77833; (979) 830-0660; www.kountryboys.com. You know a place called Kountry Boy has got to be good, and this stuff is top-notch. Using a family recipe that combines German, Polish, and Czech traditions, Kountry Boy mixes up lean cuts of meat, fresh herbs and spices, and churns them out, in natural casings and hickory smoked, for the local masses. The result is a delicious link that would be right at home on any Texas smoker. Among the sausage varieties: pork and beef without garlic, jalapeño pork and beef, pork and venison, pico de gallo, beef with garlic, and regular garlic. You can find Kountry

Boy products in more than 500 stores, including H-E-B, Kroger, Walmart, Sam's Club, and many more. All products are also available for purchase online.

La King's Confectionery, 2323 Strand, Galveston, TX 77550; (409) 762-6100; www.lakingsconfectionery.com. Oh, La King's, how I love you so. This wonderful candy and ice cream shop located in Galveston's bustling Strand district is so filled with treats that you might have a hard time getting yourself out of there. With its nearly 100 years of candy-making experience (founder Jimmy King began making candy in Houston in 1927), you know that everything that comes out of this soda shop throwback is going to be good. On one side of the store, find a functioning soda fountain serving malts, ice cream sodas, sundaes, shakes, splits, floats, fountain treats, and homemade ice cream. On the other, expect a range of fresh-made candy such as divinity, pecan pralines, hand-dipped chocolate, fudge, peanut brittle, and saltwater taffy. Special holiday-themed gift items are also available. Open daily.

Maceo Spice and Import Company, 2706 Market St., Galveston, TX 77550; (409) 763-3331; www.maceospice.com. This family-owned business has been mixing up its own spice blends for decades and now offers them for sale in its store on Market Street. Available blends include Chinese 5-spice, fajita seasoning, Greek seasoning, herbes de Provence, Honey Brown barbecue rub, jalapeño garlic salt, Jamaican jerk seasoning, seafood seasoning, taco seasoning, and a variety of salt-free options. In the store you can also find specialty food items such as pasta, imported meats and cheeses, olives, olive oils, olive salad, capers, coffee, tea, gift baskets, and more. The store also serves authentic muffalettas that you can buy and eat before or after you shop.

Old Strand Emporium, 2112 Strand, Galveston, TX 77550; (409) 515-0715; www.galveston.com/oldstrandemporium. Need something for your favorite Texas gourmand? Then pop into the Old Strand Emporium, which specializes in hard-to-find Texas foods and gifts such as hot sauces, rubs, rock candy, and wines as well as a full deli with a sandwich shop and ice cream parlor. Among my favorite items on the shelves? Wild Huckleberry Coffee and Fredericksburg Farms Sunday Haus Pancake and Waffle Mix. Oh, and don't miss the bathtub filled with wine bottles. At $6 a bottle or 3 bottles for $15, you can't go wrong. The shop is open daily year-round.

PattyCakes Bakery, 704 14th St., Galveston, TX 77550; (409) 762-2537; www.pattycakesgalveston.com. The little sister to the well-known **Mosquito Cafe** (which just so happens to be located across the street), PattyCakes Bakery opened last year and quickly became the place to go for sweet treats on the island. If you only get one thing, get the petits fours, which are melt-in-your-mouth delicious. Other menu favorites include perfectly crusty french bread, cake balls, pies, cakes, pastries, and cupcakes. Breakfast and lunch are also served. Open daily except Mon.

Food Events

Chappell Hill Lavender Festival, various locations in Chappell Hill; (979) 251-8114; www.chappellhilllavender.com. The Chappell Hill Lavender Farm, the brainchild of Jim and Debbie McDowell, is a wonderful place to visit any time of year thanks to its 23 acres of lavender loveliness. Guests at the farm may wander the acreage, enjoy lavender lemonade, pick up items such as lavender home scents, walnut face and body scrub, hand sanitizer, and bath and body products in the gift shop and even cut their own lavender for $5 a bundle. During the Chappell Hill Lavender Festival, however, the love of lavender kicks into high gear with a variety of events held throughout the town. Expect arts and crafts, food vendors, live music, hay rides, wine tasting, lavender cutting, lavender gift items, and a tour of local lavender-loving venues such as Bluebonnet House Gift and Garden Center, Lillian Farms Country Estate, and Windy Winery.

Dickens on the Strand, along the Strand in Galveston; (409) 765-7834; www.galvestonhistory.org/Dickens_Overview.asp. This incredible annual event really does bring the 19th century to life with costumed performers, live entertainment, parades, carolers, and roving street musicians who have a mission of impressing your family. Guests who come in costume receive half-price admission at the gate. And if you're a food lover, you're in luck because the vendors here are top-notch. Expect funnel cakes, hot cocoa, colossal deep-fried onions, chicken on a stick, seafood gumbo served in bread bowls, fresh-baked strudel, turkey legs, bratwurst, hot corn on the cob, cinnamon-roasted almonds, Costa Rican coffee, Scandinavian *glogg*, kettle corn, fresh-baked gingerbread cookies, hamburgers, and warm pretzels. Sure, they may not be the most authentic Victorian foods, but you're guaranteed to leave full.

Mardi Gras Galveston, various locations around town; www .mardigrasgalveseton.com. Okay, the first thing you need to know is that Galveston is home to one of the greatest Mardi Gras celebrations in the country, with more than 250,000 people attending each year. The nearly 2 weeks of festivities include a beachfront carnival, shopping, parades, major live music acts, galas, and more. What does that mean for food lovers? Lots and lots of incredible vendors, as well as specials at island restaurants.

Southwest Louisiana Boudin Trail, various spots in southwest Louisiana; www.visitlakecharles.com. You can't call yourself a true foodie until you've toured the Louisiana boudin trail, which is made up of restaurants and mom-and-pop markets along I-10 and US 90. Never heard of boudin? Pronounced "boo-dan," this local specialty looks like sausage but is filled with a mixture of ingredients such as pork, rice, onions, parsley, liver, and seasonings. The Lake Charles/Southwest Louisiana Convention and Visitors Bureau has created a self-guided tour of the best boudin joints on its website. Some of my favorite stops include **Market Basket** (4431 Nelson Rd. in Lake Charles; 337-477-4868), which looks like a dumpy little grocery store but holds some of the greatest boudin around; **Homsi's Tobacco and Beer** (2612 Kirkman St.; 337-439-2323), which sells great mild and hot traditional boudin; and **Brown's Grocery** (620 Main St. in Hackberry; 337-762-4632), where you can snag boudin balls for just 99 cents apiece and other items such as biscuits and chicken.

Cocktail Culture

Bacchus Wine Bar, 2404 Strand St., Galveston, TX 77550; (409) 765-9463; www.galveston.com/bacchus. Named for the Roman god of wine, intoxication, and debauchery, Bacchus Wine Bar has been offering all three since opening on Strand Street. Belly up to the 30-foot bar, or grab a table and take in some great live music. There's also a kitchen offering wine and food pairings. But the best part is the wine selection, which is wide and varied.

Messina Hof Winery, 4545 Old Reliance Rd., Bryan, TX 77808; (979) 778-9463; www.messinahof.com. This is actually a gold mine for both food lovers and wine lovers: There's plenty of both here to go around. Located on a 100-acre estate (42 acres of that contains the vineyard), Messina Hof has long been considered one of the greatest wineries in the state. First take a walk through the lush vineyard, then tour the winery—tours are $7 and get you 4 tastings. Popular Messina Hof wines include the Paulo Bordeaux, Paulo Cabernet Sauvignon, Unoaked Chardonnay, Sauvignon Blanc, Cabernet Franc, and "Angel" Late Harvest Riesling. Hungry? Have a seat in the Vintage House restaurant, which offers "vineyard cuisine" such as fried green tomato Napoleon, potato and vegetable pierogies, classic shrimp Creole, a Black Forest Reuben, stuffed Gorgonzola chicken, and grilled lamb chops.

Exhausted after all the wine and food? Stay overnight at the Villa at Messina Hof, which offers 10 lovely, unique rooms. There are also frequently special events at Messina Hof, including wine and food pairings, chocolate-themed nights, and harvest-related activities.

Recipes

Creamy Sopa De Poblana

For years Molina's Cantina has been a Houston institution thanks to its perfect margaritas, incredible salsas, and wonderfully cooked meats in all shapes and sizes. But what you may not realize is that the restaurant also serves up some amazing soups and salads. Among the best: the Creamy Sopa De Poblana, which has become one of the restaurant's signature dishes.

1 stick butter
⅓ cup flour
1 quart chicken stock
2¼ cups roasted, peeled, seeded and pureed poblano peppers
1 quart heavy cream
¼ cup olive oil
1¼ cup diced yellow onion

8 diced poblano peppers
6 diced red peppers
6 ears roasted fresh corn, removed from ears
1 cup chopped fresh cilantro
⅓ cup fresh lime juice
1¼ pounds jalapeño sausage, sliced and quartered
Salt and pepper to taste

Directions for base:

Melt butter in pan over medium heat.

Add flour and stir.

Add chicken stock slowly and whisk to ensure no lumps.

Add pureed poblano peppers.

Reduce heat to low and cook 15–20 minutes.

Add heavy cream and cook an additional 10 minutes, cool, strain into pot, and set aside.

Directions for vegetables:

Add olive oil to pan and heat over medium-high.

Add yellow onion and stir 1 minute.

Add poblanos, red peppers, and corn.

Cook until vegetables are soft.

Add cilantro and lime juice.

Add all to pot of poblano cream base.

Heat until soup is hot throughout.

Season with salt and pepper to taste.

Directions for serving:

Pour soup into individual bowls. Garnish with jalapeño sausage.

Makes 8 two-cup servings.

Recipe courtesy of Molina's Cantina (p. 43).

Mixed Greens with Heirloom Tomatoes, Pesto Dressing, and Pine Nuts

We've come a long way from the days when ordering a salad meant to expect a piece of lettuce and a slice of tomato on a plate. No, these days salads span the map, with ingredients that can include exotic cheeses, roasted meats, hard-to-find vegetables, and innovative dressings. Ristorante Cavour keeps it simple yet delicious with this recipe for Mixed Greens with Heirloom Tomatoes.

For the salad:

8 long, very thin slices of cucumber

6 ounces favorite salad mix

8 ounces baby heirloom tomatoes, sliced in half

4 teaspoons toasted pine nuts

4 Grissini breadsticks

For the dressing:

3 tablespoons extra-virgin olive oil

1 tablespoon Champagne vinegar

1 cup basil leaves

1 clove of garlic

1 tablespoon grated Parmesan Reggiano

Salt and pepper to taste

Place all ingredients for the dressing in a blender and blend until smooth.

Take 2 thin slices of cucumber and bend each of them into a U with the ends touching to create a shallow bowl on top of the plate.

Dress the salad and place it in the inside of the cucumber cups.

Top with tomatoes and pine nuts; garnish with a breadstick. Makes 4 servings.

Recipe courtesy of Executive Chef Renato DePirro of Ristorante Cavour (p. 52).

Crab and Shrimp Ceviche

The Cordua family is practically legendary in Houston for their wonderful restaurants, which include Churrascos, Artista, and Cordua. One of the most popular remains Americas, which serves up food-forward Latin fare. One of the restaurant's specialties is its ceviche, which is served fresh and brimming with flavor. Below, Chef David Cordua shares his recipe.

2 ounces jumbo lump crab
5 poached shrimp (directions below)
5 peeled grape tomatoes
¼ of an avocado, diced
½ ounce jalapeño
½ ounce red onion
1 ounce cilantro
2 ounces Leche de Tigre (directions below)

For poached shrimp:
½ yellow onion, chopped
3 garlic cloves
1 lemon, sliced in two
3 bay leaves
1 gallon of water
1 ounce of salt
½ pound peeled shrimp

Leche de Tigre

1 cup fresh lime juice
½ cup shrimp cooking liquid
½ cup jalapeño brine from canned jalapeños
4 garlic cloves
¼ onion

For poached shrimp:

Bring all poached shrimp ingredients to a boil in a large pot.

Add shrimp and cook for 1 minute.

Strain and cool shrimp in the fridge.

Strain and cool cooking liquid, reserving it for Leche de Tigre.

For Leche de Tigre:

Place all ingredients in a blender.

Blend for 1 minute at high.

To assemble ceviche:

In a large mixing bowl, combine all ceviche ingredients and toss in the Leche de Tigre.

Serve in a bowl with plantain or tortilla chips. Serves 1 or 2 people.

Recipe courtesy of Chef David Cordua of Americas River Oaks (p. 2).

Grilled Filet Mignon Stuffed with Caramelized Onion & Maytag Blue Cheese served with Red Wine Reduction

Sure, it's a trek to get out to Fulshear, but it's more than worth the trip to grab a bite at Ray's Grill. This unassuming "neighborhood bar and grill" prides itself on serving up dishes that incorporate seasonal and organic ingredients from local farmers. Sounds pretty good, right? The restaurant offered up this delicious filet mignon recipe.

2 filets mignon
1 cup fresh assorted herbs
5 tablespoons olive oil

Sea salt and cracked pepper to taste
2 ounces Maytag blue cheese
1 onion, caramelized

To caramelize the onion, heat 3 tablespoons olive oil in skillet. Add sliced onion and simmer until onion is soft.

For filet mignon, place herbs, remaining oil, salt, and pepper in a blender and puree until smooth. Set aside.

Make an incision in the center of the filet and stuff it with blue cheese and onion.

Pour the herb mixture over the filet mignon and marinate for about 2 hours.

Heat a skillet to high heat and sear the filet on all sides.

Finish in the oven at 425 degrees for 15 or 20 minutes.

For the red wine reduction

½ bottle of red wine
1 cinnamon stick
2 tablespoons brown sugar

Sea salt
4 ounces butter

In a sauce pan over low heat, reduce wine to one-quarter with cinnamon and sugar. Stir in butter and simmer until it reaches a sauce-like consistency. When the sauce is ready, add sea salt to taste.

Recipe courtesy of Ray's Grill (p. 133).

Lobster Mezzeluna

If you're going to book a hotel room in Houston, Hotel Derek has long been a favorite for its swanky interior and perfect location across the street from the Galleria and only a short drive from downtown. But regardless of whether you stay there, one thing you're not going to want to miss is a dinner at Valentino Vin Bar Houston, which brings Italy to life in Texas with wonderful, inspired fare. This dish for Lobster Mezzeluna comes from restaurateur Piero Selvaggio.

2 lobster tails (4 to 5 ounces each)
Extra-virgin olive oil
1 large shallot
1 tablespoon roasted garlic
2 sprigs fresh thyme

¼ cup brandy
⅓ cup mascarpone
2 cups pasta flour (finely ground flour)
1 cups blended whole eggs or ready eggs

Filling:

Clean lobster tails, then sauté the lobsters with the olive oil, shallots, roasted garlic, and thyme.

Stir the mixture often until the lobsters are almost cooked (time varies depending on the size of the lobsters), deglaze the pan with the brandy (if using an electric stove, use a lighter or match to flame the liquid after added to pan to burn off the alcohol).

Let cool, then transfer to a food processor and blend with the mascarpone cheese until smooth.

Season with salt and pepper.

Pasta:

(Note: You will need a pasta machine to make this dish.)

Add flour to bowl, mix in eggs. Blend until all of the egg is absorbed.

Transfer the dough on to a working tabletop and work until fully formed.

Wrap the mixture and let rest for 15–20 minutes.

Unwrap and make pasta sheets with your pasta machine.

Cut out circle forms in the pasta, place a small amount of the filling in the center, lightly spray with water or use egg whites to make sure the pasta stays together, then fold in a half-moon shape, pressing around the outside of the mezzeluna to ensure that it's together.

Repeat this process until all filling is gone.

Boil and serve. Makes 4 small servings.

Recipe courtesy of Valentino Vin Bar Houston (p. 65).

Grilled Rack of Lamb with Roasted New Potato & Red Currant Demi-Glace

Executive Chef Soren Pedersen has long been a fixture in the Houston restaurant scene, so it's only fitting that his Sorrel Urban Bistro opened with a great deal of buzz in summer 2011. Featuring farm-to-table fare with a new menu each week, Sorrel Urban Bistro delights diners time and time again. Here's a recipe for the restaurant's mouthwatering grilled rack of lamb.

1 rack of lamb
1 cup fresh assorted herbs

2 tablespoons olive oil
Sea salt and cracked pepper to taste

Place herbs, oil, salt, and pepper in blender and puree until smooth.

Pour the herb oil over the lamb and marinate for at least 2 hours. Place on grill at high heat and sear the rack on all sides.

Finish in oven at 425 degrees, until desired temperature.

For the Roasted Potato:

1 large Yukon Gold potato, cut into wedges

Olive oil
Salt and pepper

Toss one Yukon Gold potato, cut in wedges, with olive oil and season with salt and pepper.

Roast in baking pan at 350 degrees until tender and golden.

For the demi-glace:

3 pounds assorted veal bones
¾ pound veal leg bone
½ carrot, roughly chopped
1 small onion, roughly chopped
1 celery stalk, roughly chopped

¼ cup red Burgundy wine
1 bouquet fresh thyme
¼ teaspoon salt
3 tablespoon red currants

Preheat oven to 350 degrees. Spread bones, carrot, onion, and celery on rimmed baking sheet. Roast, tossing several times, until vegetables and bones have begun to take on color, about 1 hour.

Transfer roasted vegetables and bones to stock pot. Add wine and 2 quarts (8 cups) water and thyme and bring to boil.

Reduce heat and simmer gently until reduced to a one-quarter, about 2 hours. Strain and reserve stock.

Place stock and dried red currants in pot and reduce until sauce consistency. Stir in a few small pieces of diced cold butter before serving.

Recipe courtesy of Executive Chef Soren Pedersen of Sorrel Urban Bistro (p. 55).

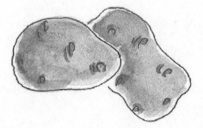

Cappellacci alla Campari

Sometimes there is nothing quite as delicious as a big, bold plate of pasta. If you're looking for a place where you can get the real deal, head to Ristorante Cavour at Hotel Granduca, where Executive Chef Renato DePirro regularly serves up favorites such as homemade gnocchi, tagliatelle, and spinach and ricotta ravioli. Want to make something that will certainly impress a date? Try out his recipe for Cappellacci alla Campari, listed below.

2 cups ricotta cheese	2 cloves garlic
1 cup steamed spinach, chopped	1 pound Campari tomatoes, wedged
1 cup grated Parmesan cheese	Salt and pepper
1 egg yolk	2 sprigs basil, chopped
12 squares fresh pasta, cooked	3 tablespoons olive oil

Filling:

In a bowl, combine ricotta, spinach, half the Parmesan, and the yolk. Season with salt and pepper.

Place about a full tablespoon of filling on the center of each square of pasta. Fold each square to make a triangle, then fold it again. Use 1 tablespoon of oil to coat the bottom of a baking sheet. Place cappellacci on baking pan. Set aside.

Sauce:

In a sauté pan, add the rest of the oil and garlic.

Let fry for a few seconds until garlic is golden, then add Campari tomatoes, salt, and pepper.

Cook at medium heat for 3 minutes, then add basil.

Pour sauce on top of cappellacci, sprinkle the rest of the Parmesan cheese, and finish in the oven for 7–8 minutes at 350 degrees. Serves 4.

Recipe courtesy of Executive Chef Renato DePirro of Ristorante Cavour (p. 52).

Chile-Rubbed Flat Iron Steak with Bacon Tomato Jam

With so many wonderful steak houses in Houston, you may wonder if it's worth the 30-minute drive out to Alvin to sample the fare of Executive Chef Jason Chaney at the Barbed Rose Steakhouse and Seafood Co. The answer to that question is a definite yes. With fresh fare that ranges from Wagyu beef to Berkshire pork, you rest assured that Chaney knows how to handle your meal. But if you'd rather cook at home, he generously offered this recipe for his Chile-Rubbed Flat Iron Steak with Bacon Tomato Jam.

- 3 tablespoons salt
- 4 teaspoons smoked sweet paprika
- 4 teaspoons dry thyme
- ½ teaspoon ground allspice
- 4 teaspoons ground white pepper
- 1 teaspoon ground cumin
- 2 teaspoons garlic powder
- 2 teaspoons onion powder
- 3 teaspoons chili powder
- 4 teaspoons cayenne pepper
- 4 teaspoons dry oregano
- 1 cup brown sugar, packed
- 2 teaspoons crushed red pepper flakes
- 2 teaspoons dry mustard
- 3 pounds flat iron steaks
- ¼ cup olive oil

Mix dry ingredients in a bowl and reserve.

Trim the flat iron of any and all sinew, and cut into portions or leave whole.

Rub the steaks with oil and season liberally with spice blend. Allow to marinate 30 minutes to 1 hour.

Cook as desired. Rest the cooked meat before slicing.

Bacon Tomato Jam

½ pound bacon, diced

2 pounds ripe tomatoes, cored
   and diced

1 yellow onion, diced

1 cup sugar

2 tablespoons cider vinegar

Salt and pepper to taste

In a large skillet over medium-high heat, cook bacon until crispy. Drain the bacon and reserve the fat for another use.

In a large saucepan, combine the tomatoes, onion, sugar, vinegar, salt, and pepper. Bring to a boil, stirring often, then reduce the heat to medium. Crumble the bacon into the tomato mixture.

Simmer until very thick. Season with salt and pepper as needed.

Chill the jam, package, and label properly.

Recipe courtesy of Executive Chef Jason Chaney
of the Barbed Rose Steakhouse and Seafood Co. (p. 145).

Chocolate Chip Cookies

Chocolate chip cookies have to be one of America's favorite guilty pleasures. Fresh baked and oozing with chocolate, there may be no better treat— no matter what time of day. I've spent a lot of time trying to find the perfect chocolate chip cookie recipe, and this one might be the best yet. You're going to want to give this recipe from Vanessa O'Donnell, who serves cookies and a host of other sweet treats such as cupcakes, cakes, and pastries at her shop, Ooh La La Dessert Boutique, a try.

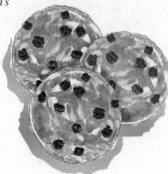

1 pound 8 ounces of butter, softened

3 cups granulated sugar

3 cups brown sugar

8 eggs

1 tablespoon plus 1 teaspoon vanilla extract

9 cups all-purpose flour

1 tablespoon plus 1 teaspoon baking soda

1 tablespoon plus 1 teaspoon salt

8 cups chocolate chips

Combine butter and both sugars in mixing bowl with paddle.

Beat at medium speed until very light and fluffy, scraping down occasionally.

Add eggs and vanilla and mix until well incorporated.

In a separate bowl, combine dry ingredients and add to above on low speed; mix just until it is completely incorporated. Be careful not to overmix.

Add chocolate chips and mix to incorporate. Cover and refrigerate dough for at least 3 hours.

Portion out cookies with an ice cream scoop.

Bake at 350 degrees for 10 minutes, turn pans, bake for an additional 10–12 minutes until golden around the edges and lighter toward the center. Makes 24 extra-large cookies.

Recipe courtesy of Vanessa O'Donnell, owner and pastry chef
of Ooh La La Dessert Boutique (p. 131).

Peach Tart Tatin

Branch Water Tavern made a huge splash in the Houston food scene when it opened in fall 2010, in large part because of Chef David Grossman's unique ability to combine classic dishes with fresh, local ingredients. The result is a place where nearly every item on the menu is sure to please, from your first appetizer to your last bite of dessert. Grossman was generous enough to offer us this recipe for his delectable Peach Tart Tatin.

5 peaches, slightly firm
1 cup sugar
¼ cup light corn syrup
1 tablespoon butter

1 sheet butter puff pastry, cut with a ring mold to the size of a pastry tatin mold
½ tablespoon salt

Score the peaches, boil them for about 5 minutes, place them in ice water, and peel them.

Halve, and remove the pits.

Combine sugar, syrup, and 4 tablespoons water in a sauce pan and cook on medium heat, stirring constantly, until the mixture takes on a brownish tint. Remove from heat and stir in butter.

Pour into foil pastry cups.

When caramel is cool, put one peach half in, cut side down, and put thirds of the other half on top. Top with a puff pastry round. Bake at 450 degrees for 12 minutes. Makes 5 servings.

Recipe courtesy of Chef David Grossman of Branch Water Tavern (p. 9).

The Big Flirt

Oh, the flirting that gets done at Monarch Restaurant and Lounge. Housed in what is arguably Houston's swankiest hotel, the Monarch draws all types of pretty people eager for a late-night dinner or a quick happy hour sipper. While a variety of delicious cocktails are available here, the Big Flirt is among my favorites for its wonderful fruity flavor—and the punch it packs.

1¼ ounces Absolut Mandrin
1¼ ounces X-Rated Fusion
Splash of pineapple juice

Splash of Champagne
Raspberry, blackberry, and
blueberry, for garnish

Combine ingredients in a shaker with ice and strain into a brown-sugar-rimmed martini glass.

Garnish with a raspberry, a blackberry, and a blueberry. Serves 1.

Recipe courtesy of Monarch Restaurant and Lounge at Hotel ZaZa (p. 44).

Sailor J's Spiced Eggnog

For Houstonians seeking a quick getaway, the San Luis Resort is a favorite, thanks to its classy vibe, upscale rooms, and fantastic Steakhouse restaurant. If you go in cooler months, the outside pool bar transforms into a winter-lover's dream, with throw blankets and drinks to warm your heart. This recipe for Sailor J's Spiced Eggnog combines three of Texans' favorite things: rum, Blue Bell ice cream, and eggnog. And because it's served cold, you can drink it any time of year.

2 ounces Sailor Jerry rum
2 ounces eggnog
1 scoop (about a ½ cup) Blue Bell vanilla ice cream

1 teaspoon ground nutmeg
Whipped cream and cinnamon stick, for garnish

Combine all ingredients in a shaker with ice, then strain into a martini glass.

Garnish with a dollop of whipped cream and a cinnamon stick. Serves 1.

Recipe courtesy of H2O Ultra-Lounge at the San Luis Resort (p. 175).

Appendix A: Eateries by Cuisine

American

Backstreet Cafe, 3

Benjy's, 5

Big Texas Dance Hall and Saloon, 160

Bistro Lancaster, 6

Black Walnut Cafe, 98

BRC Gastropub, 14

Brickhouse Tavern, 99

Cedar Creek Cafe Bar & Grill, 16

Center Court Pizza and Brew, 146

Christian's Tailgate Bar and Grill, 18

Courses Restaurant, 123

Down House, 21

Dylan's Bar and Grill, 167

Glass Wall, 25

Gravitas, 26

The Grove, 27

James Coney Island, 34

Kenny and Ziggy's Deli, 70

Little Bigs, 39

Mark's American Cuisine, 40

Monarch Restaurant and Lounge, 44

Must Be Heaven Sandwich Shop, 172

Ray's Grill, 133

RDG Bar Annie, 73

Royer's Round Top Cafe, 177

Ruggles Cafe and Bakery, 53

Ruggles Green, 135

*17 Restaurant, 53

Sorrel Urban Bistro, 55

Strata Restaurant and Bar, 105

T'Afia, 60

Tommy Bahama Restaurant
  & Store, 106

Voice Restaurant and Lounge, 66

Yard House, 139

Bakeries

The Acadian Bakery, 75

Chappell Hill Bakery and Deli, 179

Crave Cupcakes, 78
Dacapo's Pastry Cafe, 78
Elizabeth Lachlan Pastries, 108
Frost Bake Shoppe, 109
Kraftsmen Baking, 80
Moeller's Bakery, 82
Ooh La La Dessert Boutique, 131
PattyCakes Bakery, 182
Slow Dough Bread Co., 86
Sprinkles Cupcakes, 87
Sugarbaby's Cupcake Boutique, 87
Sunflower Bakery and Cafe, 175
Three Brothers Bakery, 88
The Woodlands Gourmet Bakery and
    Cafe, 111

Barbecue
Beaver's, 4
Brookstreet Barbecue, 121
Central Texas Style Barbecue, 146
Goode's Armadillo Palace, 25
Hubcap Grill, 31

Bistro Fare
Flora & Muse, 127

Breakfast
Barnaby's, 3
The Breakfast Klub, 69
Buffalo Grille, 15
Chatters Cafe and Bistro, 17
The Egg & I, 150
Egg Cetera Breakfast and Lunch
    Cafe, 100
Empire Cafe, 23
Judge Roy Bean's Coffee Saloon, 170
Mosquito Cafe, 171
Tiny Boxwood's, 63

British
Feast, 23
Queen Vic Pub & Kitchen, 51

Cajun
Boudreaux's Cajun Kitchen, 9
Cajun Greek, 165
Mardi Gras Grill, 40

Caribbean
D Caribbean Curry Spot, 150

Chinese
Fung's Kitchen, 128
HK Dim Sum, 128

Ocean Palace Restaurant, 130

Cocktail Lounges
Anvil Bar and Refuge, 93
Beaver's, 4, 94

Cuban
El Meson Cuban Restaurant, 22

European
Eatcetera, 167

French
Aura Restaurant, 118
Bistro Alex, 120
Brasserie Max and Julie, 12
Brasserie 19, 13
Cafe Moustache, 15
Chez Roux, 99
Mockingbird Bistro, 42
Philippe's Restaurant, 49

German
Rudi Lechner's Restaurant and
    Bar, 134

Greek
Mediterraneo Market and Cafe, 154

Niko Niko's, 71
Olympia Grill, 173

Indian
Bombay Brasserie, 7
Bombay Pizza Co., 7
India's Restaurant, 129
Indika, 33
Khyber North Indian Grill, 37
Pondicheri, 50
Queen Vic Pub & Kitchen, 51
Udipi Cafe, 138

Italian
Brio Tuscan Grille, 121
Candelari's Pizza, 123
D'Amico's Italian Market Cafe, 19
Dibella's Italian Restaurant, 166
Grotto, 101
La Griglia, 37
Mario's Italian Ristorante, 171
Ristorante Cavour, 52
Spaghetti Western Italian Cafe, 56
Star Pizza, 57
Stella Sola, 58
Tavola Tuscan Bistro, 106
Tony's, 74
Trattoria Il Mulino, 138

Valentino Vin Bar Houston, 65

Japanese
Azuma Sushi and Robata Bar, 119
Ichiban Sushi & Tapioca, 129
Little Tokyo, 153
Masa Sushi Japanese Restaurant, 153
RA Sushi, 132
Sushi Raku, 59
Uni Sushi, 107

Latin American
Americas, 2

Meat Markets
Burton Sausage Company, 178
Chappell Hill Sausage Company, 179
Eckermann's Meat Market, 180
Hebert's Specialty Meats, 109
Kountry Boy Sausage, 180
Oaxaca Meat Market, 157
Southwest Louisiana Boudin
    Trail, 184
Veron's Cajun Meat Market, 110

Mexican
Pico's Mex-Mex, 50
Tila's Restaurant and Bar, 62

Seafood
Benno's on the Beach, 164
Casey's Seafood Cafe, 166
Danton's Gulf Coast Seafood
    Kitchen, 20
Eddie V's Prime Seafood, 126
Fisherman's Wharf, 168
Floyd's Cajun Seafood and Texas
    Steakhouse, 151
Gaido's Seafood Restaurant, 169
Gilhooley's Restaurant and Oyster
    Bar, 152
O'Cajcen Seafood Restaurant, 154
Oceanaire Seafood Room, 45
Pesce, 48
Reef, 51
Shrimp and Stuff, 174
Sudie's Seafood House, 156
Willie G's Steakhouse and
    Seafood, 67

Singaporean
Straits Restaurant, 135

Southern
Bernardo's Restaurant, 165
Big Woodrow's, 119
Boondoggles Pub and Pizzeria, 161

Hugo's, 70
Irma's Houston, 34
Lupe Tortilla Mexican
     Restaurant, 102
Molina's Cantina, 43
The Original Ninfa's on
     Navigation, 72
Tacos a Go Go, 60

Thai
Khun Kay Thai, 36
Nit Noi Thai, 104
Thai Cottage, 136

24-Hour Dining
59 Diner, 126
House of Pies, 30
Katz's Deli and Bar, 36
One's a Meal Greek Village, 46
Spanish Flower Mexican
     Restaurant, 56

Vegetarian
Blue Nile Ethiopian Restaurant, 120
Field of Greens, 24
Hobbit Cafe, 30

Vietnamese
Huynh Restaurant, 32
Jenni's Noodle House, 35
Kim Son, 130
Les Givral's Kahve. 39
Mai's, 71

Wine Bars
Allegria Wine Bar and Cocktail
     Lounge, 160
Bacchus Wine Bar, 185
Block 7 Wine Company, 94
Boom Boom Room, 8
Cha Champagne and Wine Bar, 95
Chelsea Wine Bar, 161
CRU, 114
Crush Wine Lounge, 115
Haak Vineyards & Winery, 162
Messina Hof Winery, 186
The Tasting Room–Uptown Park, 96
WineStyles The Vintage, 116

Appendix B: Dishes, Specialties & Specialty Food

Willie G's Steakhouse and
Seafood, 67

Hamburgers
Aura Restaurant, 118
Barbed Rose Steakhouse and
Seafood Co., 145
Cajun Greek, 165
Casey's Seafood Cafe, 166
Cedar Creek Cafe Bar & Grill, 16
Christian's Tailgate Bar and
Grill, 18
Lankford Market, 38
Little Bigs, 39
Oaxaca Meat Market, 157
Tommy Bahama Restaurant and
Store, 106
Yaga's Cafe, 176

Happy Hour
Allegria Wine Bar and Cocktail
Lounge, 160
*17 Restaurant, 53
Strata Restaurant and Bar, 105

Hot Dogs
James Coney Island, 34

Ice Cream
Marble Slab Creamery, 81

Pasta
Brio Tuscan Grille, 121
Dibella's Italian Restaurant, 166
Grotto, 101
Peppers Beef & Seafood, 155
Spaghetti Western Italian Cafe, 56
Tavola Tuscan Bistro, 106
Trattoria Il Mulino, 138

Pastries & Sweets
Blue Bell Creamery, 177
Chappell Hill Bakery and Deli, 179
The Chocolate Bar, 77
Cleburne Cafeteria, 18
Dacapo's Pastry Cafe, 78
Empire Cafe, 23
House of Pies, 30
La King's Confectionery, 181
Mo's... A Place for Steaks, 44
Moeller's Bakery, 82
Must Be Heaven Sandwich
Shop, 172
One Green Street, 83
PattyCakes Bakery, 182

Pie in the Sky Pie Co., 84
Pondicheri, 50
Royer's Round Top Cafe, 177
Ruggles Cafe and Bakery, 53
Strip House, 59
Tiny Boxwood's, 63
Three Brothers Bakery, 88
The Woodlands Gourmet Bakery and
    Cafe, 111

Pho
Huynh Restaurant, 32
Jenni's Noodle House, 35

Pizza
Bombay Pizza Co., 7
Boondoggles Pub and Pizzeria, 161
Candelari's Pizza, 123
Center Court Pizza and Brew, 146
Crush Wine Lounge, 115
D Caribbean Curry Spot, 150
Mario's Italian Ristorante, 171
Star Pizza, 57

Pub Grub
Brickhouse Tavern, 99
Dylan's Bar and Grill, 167

Goose's Acre Bistro and Irish
    Pub, 115
Yard House, 139

Quesadillas
Cyclone Anaya's Mexican
    Kitchen, 125
Lupe Tortilla Mexican
    Restaurant, 102
Molina's Cantina, 43
The Original Ninfa's on
    Navigation, 72
Spanish Flower Mexican
    Restaurant, 56

Sandwiches
Boom Boom Room, 8
Brookstreet Barbecue, 121
Central Texas Style Barbecue, 146
D'Amico's Italian Market Cafe, 19
Eatcetera, 167
Goode's Armadillo Palace, 25
The Grove, 27
Katz's Deli and Bar, 36
Kenny and Ziggy's Deli, 70
Kraftsmen Baking, 80
Les Givral's Kahve, 39

Index